PATTAYA
2020

PATTAYA 2020

Phil Hall

Copyright © 2020 Phil Hall
All rights reserved.

Cover design and back cover photo by Matt Lawrence - mattlawrence.net

No part of this book may be reproduced or transmitted in any form or by any means, graphic, electronic, or mechanical, including photocopying, recording, taping, or by any information storage retrieval system, without the permission, in writing, from the publisher.

CONTENTS

So It Begins... 7
The Morning After 42
Reality Bites 63
Swift return 79
Revenge is a dish best served by a Ladyboy 101
How the mighty have fallen 109
Delightful Debs 121
Chilli returns 141
Christmas Eve 154
Christmas Day 161
End Game 184
Epilogue 192
Appendix 194
Thank you 214
Author's Note 216

Chapter One
SO IT BEGINS...

Her room was just like the hundreds of others in this rundown apartment block. Small and stuffy and hot as hell most of the time. The ceiling fan was pretty useless, it only served to circulate the stifling air and sounded as if it would come apart at any moment.

The girl in the mirror was very pretty and had a smile that could stop a bullet in its tracks. Her family used to say that she could have been a model, if only she had been taller. Less than five feet in her high heels, she was barely 43 kilograms soaking wet, but had an attitude that warned much bigger people not to mess with her.

'Mah see mair mung!' Thai for 'your mother fucks dogs!' These words left her beautiful mouth as she cursed a mosquito who dared to land on her perfect skin.

She was getting ready to leave for work. Her shift started at 8pm and wouldn't finish until the sun came up over the South China Sea.

She moved to Pattaya a few years ago and was earning more money than she had ever dreamed possible. Sleeping with farangs wasn't so bad as she had first thought. Most of them were polite enough but she worried that the really big ones would roll over onto her in the night and crush her tiny frame to death. So far that hadn't happened but she always slept with one eye open just in case.

Most of her money was sent back to her home in Isaan and it was helping to put her younger sister through university.

Like most bar girls, she referred to her customers as 'it' (Mun). This amused her at first because in her eyes some of these weren't really anything better than animals, buffalos if you will. They usually wanted

So It Begins...

to have sex as soon as they got to their hotel room. If she was lucky, it wouldn't last very long. Then again in the morning, usually even quicker this time around.

But, like many working girls in Pattaya, she had discovered that only a minority of these men were in that category. Many of them had good hearts and it was quite possible to have a girlfriend relationship with these foreign men. Occasionally, she would even start to fall for one or two, but they never stayed long enough to take things to the next level.

Probably for the best.

She looked in the mirror and made a silent prayer to Buddha, hoping against hope that tonight would be the one where a handsome young stranger came to her bar. Of course, he would also be very rich and it would be love at first sight for both of them. She blew herself a little kiss and turned on her heel towards the door.

Her name was Ice, if only she could be as cool when dealing with matters of the heart.

* * *

Some 6000 miles to the West of Ice's apartment, 3 hungover men were boarding a Thai Airways flight bound for Bangkok. All were in their mid-thirties with a thick Oxfordshire accent, and despite their raging headaches, they seemed in high spirits. Leaving the miserable UK in April for the promise of some warm weather and even hotter women, who wouldn't be feeling good?

'I can't wait to get some of that Thai pussy!'

Chilli was rubbing his hands with glee and his evil chuckle made the nearby flight attendant shiver with repulsion. He didn't give a toss, never did. This lad pleased himself. This was going to be one hell of a shag fest and his two companions could like it or lump it.

'Remember - there'll be no photos or Facebook updates or my bollocks are going to be sliced off as soon as I get home!'

Chilli smiled even more and wondered how in the hell Jack had managed to convince his fiancée-to be that they were flying to Benidorm for his impromptu stag do, not Thailand. Of course, there was always the possibility that she'd check his passport stamps in the future but that was Jack's problem, not his.

'Fucking hell there's no leg room in these seats.'

Shaun was the biggest drinker in the group and standing at over 6 feet 5, they said he must have hollow legs. This trip was his idea and he had been looking forward to it even more than Chilli, albeit for very different reasons.

A few hours into the flight and they were back on the piss and the beers were flowing just as they did the night before. You had to feel sorry for the passengers in the surrounding seats because this bunch were not letting anybody sleep, not a chance! But eventually, they ran out of stamina and were snoring and farting like a bunch of pre-spit roast pigs.

Because of his height, Shaun had an arm and a leg stretched across the aisle and one of the flight attendants was enjoying smashing the heavy food trolley into his limbs on more than one occasion.

Jack woke up first and looked at his ramshackle party wondering why the hell he had even come along on this trip. Okay, he wasn't head over heels in love with Debs, but she was a decent enough catch. At 35 years old, he wouldn't get anything better.

Still, this trip was a pretty shitty act and he felt guilty as fuck when he lied regarding the true destination.

To make matters worse, Shaun, who had planned the whole event was his future brother-in-law. What would happen if they fell out one day? The lanky bastard would have him over a barrel.

So It Begins...

'First time is it lads?'

Jack felt his chair lurch backwards as the head and shoulders of a man well into his 60's appeared between him and Chilli.

'Yeah that's right, why do you ask?'

Not one for sharing information, Jack was naturally cautious, but the old boy had a friendly smile and wasted no time introducing himself.

'I'm Frank and this is my 40th trip to Thailand'.

Chilli and Shaun were soon all ears, and the novice trio listened as he regaled them with his experiences in Bangkok, Pattaya and loads of other places they'd never heard of.

'Where are you three boys staying?'

Shaun had booked the trip but couldn't even remember the name of the hotel.

'Somewhere in Pattaya'.

'Well, that's the place to go boys. You are going to have the time of your lives. I'm staying on Soi 6, that's the best part of the town. It's impossible to walk from one end to the other without being dragged into a bar by some gorgeous ladies'.

'I'll have some of that!'

Chilli's eyes were almost bulging out of his head at the thought of this.

'Come out with me tonight and I'll show you the best bars in Pattaya'.

There was no stopping this old boy, he handed over a business card with a photo of a much younger version of him embossed on the front.

'I'll meet you in Soi 6 tonight, my favourite bar is Envy and I'll be the one surrounded by the best looking birds.'

'How the fuck will an old cunt like you manage that?' Shaun blurted out.

Instead of taking offence, Frank just laughed and sat back down in his chair.

'In Pattaya, I'm a hansum man'.

Frank continued

'Back in the UK nobody notices me, especially the ladies. In Thailand, I can strut around like a 2 week millionaire, but remember lads….'

He paused for dramatic effect and delivered his well-worn punchline:

'No money, no honey!'

The three Wallingford would-be lotharios laughed awkwardly and went back to their beers.

Jack was wondering what lay ahead. Would he be able to rise to the occasion even though he was supposed to get married in a matter of weeks?

Quite a few hours later, as the plane touched down at Suvarnabhumi airport, he glanced out of the window to see a bright yellow sun staring right back at him. He felt an involuntary shudder and started to brace himself for the experience of a lifetime.

* * *

Tonight was a slow one for Ice. She had worn a short skirt and had her lovely hair tied back to show off her high cheekbones, but even that wasn't enough to attract a single customer to her bar.

The other five girls were asleep under the counter and they had long given up the ghost. Typically, a beer bar would have a number of 'retainer' girls who were well past their sell by date. They always turned up for work on time and because the customers weren't remotely interested in bar fining them, they were stalwarts that could be depended on.

On the other hand, Ice was the star of Porn Bar Number 5, and was usually in demand. But tonight was pretty dead and even the livelier bars near the Beach road were struggling to pull in the punters. It was only

So It Begins...

1am and if things didn't pick up, she'd have another five or six hours of boredom before going back to her shit hole of a room.

Was this the future her parents had wanted for her when they worked their fingers to the bone on that rice farm back in Buriram? In this developing country, what other choices did she have? At least she was contributing to her family now, and despite the fact she was selling her body to the highest bidder, it was better than scraping a living selling noodles or working in a bloody factory on twelve-hour shifts.

'Excuse me dear?'

She looked up and tried not to flinch because one of the fattest men she had ever seen was sitting across the bar from her. She got him a beer and allowed the man to paw at her lovely skin as he drooled like a salivating pig.

Twenty minutes later Ice was back at the man's hotel and she looked in the mirror wondering why the fuck she'd bothered praying to Buddha after all. He never listened and if he did, he was pissing himself with laughter right now. At least this one was taking a shower.

As he came back onto the bed, she closed her eyes and thought of her younger sister at University and started to do what she did best.

* * *

'Sir, what is your reason for coming to Thailand?'

'To shag your Mum'.

He grinned at the immigration official who merely stamped his passport and waved him through. Not quite the response he'd expected but the poor lad had heard this shit hundreds of times.

Chilli was a joker but he was also a bit of an adrenalin junkie who grew bored quickly. At school the teachers had thought he suffered from some advanced form of ADHD but after extensive tests, it was clear he was just a busy little cunt.

Chilli was always the first one to start trouble of any kind, and as Jack watched him swagger through to the baggage carousel, he wondered why they had even invited him? He knew that Thailand was a place where bad shit happened to foreigners looking for it and here was a prime example of the idiots featured on 'Brits banged up abroad'.

Meanwhile twenty paces behind him, Shaun was stressing out about the fact he'd left his duty free back on the plane.

'I forked out a small fortune for that Hugo Boss perfume and now I've fucking forgotten it!'

Chilli picked up on his stress and was typically unsympathetic.

'Shaun you lanky streak of cat's piss, who the hell buys perfume on a trip to Thailand?'

He muttered something regarding a present for his Nan but by now their suitcases had appeared on the carousel and it was time for them to man up and walk through the customs channels. This proved to be eventless and in contrast to Heathrow, there wasn't a single officer to be found.

'Hey Shaun, where was it you said we were going?'

As they approached the arrivals hall, there was a sea of Asian faces and they were all holding name cards. Shaun had stopped in his tracks and was surveying the scene intently.

'There we go!'

He marched directly up to a uniformed Thai chap and the rest of the group had to laugh when they saw the sign he was happily waving for all to see. It read

'Wallingford Massive on Tour'.

Fair enough really. But, apart from Jack, they were all single, pretty much desperate and not remotely Massive in any way.

So It Begins...

It was a surprise that none of them had ever ventured to Thailand before. Despite the hype, the place to be wasn't Bangkok, instead it was a seaside town called Pattaya. None of them had even heard of the place but a little searching on the internet had certainly removed any doubts that this was the place to go.

Jack's phone started buzzing and as his roaming sim card connected with the local network, he grimaced inwardly as he read the text message from Debs.

'How are you enjoying Benidorm, darling?'

'Fucking hell...'

If he hadn't realised before how destructive this lie had been, he certainly did now.

The next thing he knew, she was trying to start a Messenger chat! As if by instinct, he pressed the power button for a few seconds and looked around for some support.

Shaun started to giggle and then his bloody phone started buzzing as well. He smiled at Jack and looked as if he was going to answer the bloody thing.

'I'm only messing you soft twat!' At that moment, he knew that this trip was one big fucking mistake.

* * *

In the morning Ice shook the man mountain for at least ten minutes before he woke up with a huge fart. The stench was horrible but she kept smiling and kissed the man whilst praying that he'd be too tired for morning sex. He rolled over, grabbed a fistful of Thai notes and simply threw them in her direction.

'What a rude bastard'

She whispered sweetly in Thai, as she grasped the money. Ice didn't bother showering just in case he had a change of heart. Twenty minutes later she was back at home and spent the next hour in the shower washing away the smell of that foul creature.

Dripping wet and without her towel on, Ice looked in that mirror as she had done the night before. This time no prayers were uttered. She knew that this was how it was going to be. Well at least until her looks started to fade. She'd end up like the hundreds of freelancers that were too old to work bars and spend her time hustling customers as they walked along the beach road in the evening.

In a rare moment of clarity, she threw herself on the bed and start sobbing her heart out. How had she become this wreck? Why had her Thai boyfriend treated her like shit all those years ago? He was sweet enough in the beginning, until he started gambling and cheating on her. Then the beatings came and that was the last straw. The day he broke her nose, Ice knew that she had to go.

She left the village and got a job at the Buriram Tawen Daeng as a server. It was fun but she hated being pawed by the older customers. Her friend offered her a way out of Isaan and invited her to come and work in Pattaya. And here she was.

Ice turned on the ceiling fan and tried her best to sleep, praying that the huge spinning device would somehow transport her back in time. To a happier place. But she knew that was not on the cards.

* * *

They say that New York is the city that never sleeps, if that's the case, Pattaya is the city that is always having a 24/7 party.

The lads' taxi took them there in less than two hours and they were staying in the Eastiny Inn hotel in Soi 8. Typical of Pattaya's budget hotels, it had seen better days but was still popular thanks to a low price and it was 'Guest Friendly'

So It Begins...

Pattaya has literally hundreds of hotels ranging from seedy hostels to five-star luxury venues. The cheaper ones would allow their patrons to bring a bar girl back to the room, although some would charge a fee, they would also check her ID. This was an insurance policy to protect them and their guests against theft or even worse.

Shaun had read up on this, hence the Eastiny Inn was chosen. It was now around 4pm and the place was already teeming with life.

For those who aren't familiar with this town/city, Soi 8 is one of the little streets that connects the main Beach road to the almost as busy second road. Some of these streets, or Sois, are fairly laid back. This is not one of those...

'Fuck me lads, look at the pussy out there!'

The taxi driver smiled as he could see the three excited faces in his rear-view mirror. He never grew bored of seeing grown men act like children around these bars, not that he blamed them. Many was the time he spent a few hours on his back as a much younger countrywoman tended to his every dirty little need.

They piled out of the taxi and Chilli was already making his way to one of the bars opposite the hotel as Jack and Shaun paid the taxi driver in the confusing Thai currency.

'Oi you dirty bastard, let's at least check into the hotel first!'

But it was no good, Chilli had already ordered his first beer and was eyeing up the bar staff like an eagle checking out a field of new born rabbits. Less than 15 minutes later, they joined him.

'What the fuck am I going to say to Debs?'

Shaun still had that shit eating grin on his face.

'Mate, if you really loved her, would you even be here?'

He had a valid point.

So It Begins...

Jack knocked back his first beer and tried to wipe away any guilt as he looked around, for the first time, at this new and exotic environment. Well, there were certainly a lot of pretty ladies to be seen, that was in no doubt. Each of the small bars that he could see housed around twelve of these delightful looking hostesses and, try as he might, he couldn't spot a single munter amongst them.

He ordered a second beer and was surprised that instead of taking his money, another chit appeared in the little wooden vessel in front of him. The beers were around £2 each and they tasted as good as anything back in Wallingford.

The others were engaged with their own personal hostess and as Chilli started taking photos with his phone, Jack's heart sank a little.

'For fucks sake, don't upload them pictures you dozy tit! We're supposed to be in Spain, not fucking Pattaya!'

Chilli smirked and carried on taking snaps.

'Stop being a wet blanket, fella, they're for my own personal wank collection'.

He sniggered and eventually put the device away as he got stuck into a game of Connect 4 with his new best friend.

* * *

Tonight was as slow as it gets for Ice and the rest of the crew at Porn Bar Number 5. She'd given up hope of anything happening and started tucking into a bowl of Mama noodles. Costing less than twenty pence in Thai money, they really were the staple diet of Pattaya's night workers. Known simply as 'The Industry', there must have been 25,000 souls at any point in time, earning their money in the world's oldest profession.

'Ice, the boss has asked for you to go to her second bar, it's busy and lots of customers are looking for girls.'

So It Begins...

To be honest, even though she could have done with some money, right now Ice would have been happier staying put just eating noodles. But the Boss was a fierce lady and her bite was worse than her bark. So, she gobbled them up, waied to the spirit house at the front of Porn Bar Number 5, and hailed a motorbike taxi to get her to her destination.

Five minute later, she was on Soi 8 and was surprised to see that the bar was actually busy.

She wasted no time in helping out by serving a couple of men their beers. She looked at both of them and they were already in the arms of two ladies. She didn't care because one was already kissing the face off her associate and the other one had a strange look on his face, as if he was on drugs.

She had a few minutes to get her bearings and then she noticed him. This man looked to be around 35 years old and, although he was not particularly handsome, he had a nice smile and wasn't brash like most of the drunken foreigners around him.

Jack was still worried about his phone ringing and couldn't get into the Pattaya party mode just yet, unlike his two travelling buddies. Jesus Christ, they were all on a fucking mission and he'd never seen them looking so happy.

He had to admit it, Thai ladies were bloody gorgeous and their slim bodies were nothing like the women back home. They all had their own style and, after checking his phone, when he looked up, he saw the most beautiful face looking directly at him.

What an absolute peach!

She held his gaze for ten seconds and when she eventually looked away, he was sweating as if he'd ran a mile in four minutes. He got distracted and suddenly she was out of sight.

Shaun had noticed, being a sly little weasel and started taking the piss

'Fancy her, do you? Remember Jack, they are all available – fuck - I could have her if I wanted'.

Jack fancied her a lot and the idea of Shaun coming near this vision made him almost retch.

There was a tap on his shoulder and he swung round to see this Thai Angel beaming right at him.

'Mister, would you like a drink?'

Her voice was heavily accented and Jack could detect what he thought were a bout of nerves. Surely not? These girls were professionals and she was probably just putting on an act.

He asked for a Singha beer and offered to buy her one as well. Her gorgeous almond eyes widened as she scurried off to get the drinks.

Then his phone started ringing again and he realised that Shaun must have turned the fucking thing back on. What a bell end…

Ice had cheered up; this man had already won her over with his honest and open smile and deep blue eyes. Perhaps she fell in love too easily but that was her business. Ice wasn't jaded like most of the girls in this city and She was going to try and see if this potential customer could develop into something more.

Ice rushed back with the two beers and he'd even pulled a chair out for her to sit down. What a gentleman! They drank the cool beers in unison and she took his free hand and placed it on her bare thigh. At first the man seemed a little nervous, this was a pleasant surprise. Then he squeezed her just right and Ice started to feel a little lightheaded herself. This could be a very good night!

Jack was on his fourth beer and realised that the girl was now sat on his lap.

Shaun and Chilli had left 30 minutes ago. They were off to link up with Frank, the old geezer from the flight. He had no interest in joining them for now and was enjoying the company of this beautiful creature. Her name was Ice, she had perfect teeth and skin as soft as silk. Every time she touched him, he could feel some electricity flowing through his body, in particular his groin area!

It was different with the woman he had left at home. Debs wasn't an oil painting and she had a legendary temper, but would hopefully offer him a solid basis for starting a new family. Jack was bad with money and had run up some serious debts by the time he was 30 years old. Moving from bedsit to ropey old bedsit, it was unlikely that he would ever own property. In some ways, Debs was the perfect 'out' from this miserable existence. She already had her own house and a healthy income. She earnt triple his measly salary and was extremely thrifty.

So why was he here? Well, the electricity he was feeling with Ice was something he never experienced with the hot headed and wealthier Debs. Had he been missing this feeling most of his life? Probably…

'Cheers!'

They touched beer bottles together as another round was bought.

She was very close to him by now and when she leant in for a kiss, Jack thought why the fuck not? Just as they touched lips, his groin started to actually vibrate. His bloody phone was on silent and somebody was ruining this perfect moment. He pulled back and removed the device from his pocket and cursed inwardly as he realised that Debs wasn't giving up. He placed it on the bar and that was when everything started to fall apart.

Ice couldn't remember when she last felt this relaxed with anyone, let alone a customer. This man smelt really good and had a very light yet warm touch. In fact, every time he squeezed her, she had goose bumps all over her skin. This was new territory for her. She wanted him and she was going to fucking have him.

So It Begins…

Hell, she would fuck this one for free if she didn't need the money so bad. Her parents had asked for more this month and she was their main source of income.

He looked keen but would he want to pay her for her services? There was one way to find out. She leant in for a kiss and just as she was going to slip her tongue in his mouth, the man pulled back. That wasn't how it was meant to work out. He pulled a cell phone out of his pocket and placed it carefully on the bar. It was vibrating like mad and looked as if it might even fall off onto the floor. Ice reached over to move it away from the ledge and then something happened that fucked up the whole experience.

'Don't touch my phone you stupid fucking bitch!'

As soon as those words left his mouth, he instantly knew that he'd screwed up big time. Despite the language barrier, this girl knew that he was cursing her and his body language removed any doubts that she was harbouring. She fixed him with a steely gaze and in an instant, she had gone.

Jack had snapped because for some reason he thought Ice was going to answer the phone and speak to Debs. What a retard… The mobile eventually stopped ringing, and Jack looked around to see if Ice was lurking nearby. She wasn't anywhere to be seen. He was furious, not because he'd almost been caught out telling the world's biggest lie to Debs. Not because he'd just missed out on the chance to have sex with the most perfect girl he'd ever seen. No.

He was mad at himself because he cared so much. There must be over 20,000 girls in this fucking place and to quote his soon to be brother in law:

'They are all available'.

But he knew, this girl wasn't the same. Not for him.

Again, the sodding phone started to ring. This time he manned up and answered it.

So It Begins...

Ice was in tears almost ten minutes after that man had been such an arse. He had no right to speak to her like that. Maybe her friends were right, these farangs were just buffalos and were not to be trusted, not ever. Was her judgement so bad that she allowed herself to believe this one was any different?

Her boss was calling her cell phone but she just couldn't deal with that bitch right now. She'd lose her night's pay but she would prefer to be just be alone. Why couldn't she be a hard faced cow like all of the other working girls?

Checking her purse Ice was surprised to find a 500 baht note crumpled up in the corner. This was a result! She stopped at the 7-11 shop and spent half of it on a small bottle of Sang Som. The Thai rum that had ruined many a marriage and this would at least help to block out any false hope that she harboured for that stupid man.

Five minutes later she was sat on her mattress and as she opened the screw top, she looked in the mirror and couldn't even bring herself to look away as she slowly brought the bottle of spirits to her lips.

* * *

'Finally babes, you managed to take my call!'

Jack steeled himself for what was coming and he wasn't disappointed.

'We're at the airport and we'll be with you in four hours!'

Her excited voice rang through his ears, this couldn't be true, surely not? She was en route to Benidorm and expecting a reunion... Except he was over 6000 miles away from that dump.

He did the maths. Even if he had managed to get on a plane right away, he'd take more than 12 hours to reach Spain. He doubted there were any direct flights to Benidorm.

'Well, what do you say?'

It was too much. He turned the phone off and admitted defeat.

The wedding was never going to happen. Surely Shaun knew this before they'd even got on the plane. The prick had stitched him up like a smoked kipper. After five minutes of self-pity, Jack got up and walked away from the bar.

'Mister, Mister, you have to pay your bill!'

The haggard server grabbed him by the arm with a surprisingly strong grip and held out her hand. He paid the bar lady, could hardly call her a girl, and walked off to nowhere in particular. All he felt like doing right now was finding Shaun and punching his fucking lights out. Then he'd find that lovely Ice and do what needed doing.

Halfway down the Soi he saw a slim Thai lady sitting alone outside a small bar. Was it Ice?

His heart skipped a beat and he sprinted over to her. She turned around with a scowl and he realised she was nothing like his special lady.

'Hey, come and sit down'

She called after Jack. But he was off again.

He reached the beach road and was surprised to find out that there were bars as far as the eye could see. After passing what seemed like dozens, he gave in to the constant cat calls and plonked himself down on a bar stool. Instead of beer, he ordered a double JD and Coke, despite knowing how fucked up this stuff made him feel. Four or five doubles later and the other Jack was feeling just fine!

After settling his bill, he stumbled across the busy street, narrowly avoiding a motorbike. The beach road was full of bars on one side and the left, well it was the beach… Soon he noticed that the emptier side was full of ladies of all shapes and sizes. They were freelancers. These were prostitutes that didn't work at bars. Some of them had day jobs and a few were even students, trying to earn an extra thousand baht or more.

So It Begins...

Okay, those unfamiliar with Thailand may think that all sex workers are cut from the same cloth. Not at all. Each bar girl is loyal to her own establishment and should they upset or steal from a paying customer, the bar owner or mamasan will dish out a punishment that will not be forgotten in a hurry. The problem could attract police and the business could suffer as a result. No such issues for the freelancers. These ladies could rob a punter blind and then go underground for a few days, reappearing on the beach strip ready to start all over again.

Poor Jack wasn't to know this. They certainly looked mighty fine. Especially after those double bourbons he had been putting away. He'd all but forgotten about Debs and his fucked-up future. Couldn't quite drink away Ice though.

'1000 baht and I fuck you all night'.

Turning around, Jack saw a slim thirty-something Thai lady with a huge smile and he could smell her perfume before he could respond. She moved in for the kill and within seconds the dark-skinned beauty already had her hand down his pants.

'Why the hell not?'

He said out aloud and returned the compliment, pulling her towards him and shoving his whisky laced tongue into her mouth.

* * *

A few hours earlier, Shaun and Chilli were struggling to find Soi 6 and, along the way, they'd enjoyed drinking in the sights of Pattaya during high season.

One week earlier had been the Thai New Year and this is a festival that needs to be seen to be believed. From around the 13th of April, in Pattaya, the whole pace is turned into an utterly mental water throwing party for a whole seven days. It's 24/7 and locals as well as tourists soak each other whilst getting smashed on their favourite tipple.

Some of the grumpier residents even move out of the town for the week as they absolutely hate the soaking that they receive every time they leave the safety of their apartment/hotel/house. It's a wonder why they ever moved in Pattaya in the first place but some people, as you know, they aren't happy unless they are miserable.

The pair wandered along the Beach Road from the top of Soi 8 and once they'd navigated their way across the Central Road by Soi 7, they started to think that they were going the wrong way. Passing the Hard Rock Hotel, the bars on the beach road started to become scarcer and just as Shaun was going to suggest they go back, Chilli who was ten yards ahead, turned around and said,

'Oh Sweet Jesus!'

He was looking directly down a small road that was buzzing with lights and swarming with life.

Shaun quickly caught up and the pair of them stood there for a minute before they came to their senses. The small road was packed with bars as far as they could see and each one had at least 20 scantily clad beauties scampering around the front.

'Soi 6, I fucking love it!'

Chilli led the way and as soon as he had reached the first bar, he disappeared from Shaun's sight and it was as if he'd never been there.

Shaun bravely took a few more steps and then he was grabbed by at least three different girls at once.

'Hello handsome man! You want to buy me a drink?'

He looked at the six-armed beast that was pulling him towards the first bar and was met with 3 golden brown and beautiful cheeky faces, all grinning from ear to ear. They smelt so good.

Then a further pair of hands grabbed his groin and Shaun was in paradise.

So It Begins...

Inside the bar it was fairly dark and Chilli was already on a huge leather sofa surrounded by his posse of hotties. Shaun was dragged to the next sofa and ordered a round of drinks. The bill came with them, but he was too horny to even take a look. One of the girls was literally straddling him and his pulse was racing as if he'd just ran a fucking marathon.

'That old cunt was right; I feel like a millionaire already'

Chilli shouted out, but Shaun wasn't listening. He was already halfway up the stairs to continue his 'conversation' with the beautiful 'straddler' whose name was 'Nung'. This was Thai for 'One'. 'Well', thought Shaun, 'I'm giving her one tonight'

An hour later, both utterly relaxed, the pair of Romeos managed to find Envy Bar and started looking for Frank. Once more, they were dragged willingly into the place and were being manhandled by a group of fit ladies as they tried, in vain, to track down their would-be mentor.

Chilli flashed the man's business card to any girl within earshot and asked them, 'Have you seen this man?'

The typical reply was a shake of the head followed by,

'You buy drink for me, na darling?'

He'd got the same answer at least five times and had all but given up when a particularly pretty one with huge tits caught his eye. She beckoned him to come over as if he was a naughty pup and before he could repeat the question, she placed a slender finger on his lips and shoving his hand down the front of her tiny shorts, asked him:

'Have you seen this pussy?'

Then, placing his, now moist fingers, back into his mouth, before he could even think of answer, she pulled him onto her lap and started to kiss him all over whilst sniffing him like a proud mother would a newly born baby.

So It Begins...

The Thai Kiss, also known as 'Hom Noi' is a combination of sniffing and kissing that is unique to Thailand

Both lads were on their second or third beer when about 20 fairly pissed revellers made their presence known.

The oldest of the bunch marched straight up to a huge bell hanging over the main bar and started ringing it like a man possessed.

This caused shit loads of interest and the whole bar started chanting in unison 'Frank! Frank! Frank!'

Yep, you guessed it, the lads had found their man.

Beers where bought for everyone in the place and a few more besides that must have heard the ringing from outside.

Frank was properly living it large and introduced the bar crawl organiser to them.

'Guys, this is Mister Bryan Flowers and he's the fucking man in this part of the world!'

Chilli and Shaun shook hands and listened as Frank explained that Bryan was the CEO of a company called Night Wish Group. Chilli looked as if he would explode with jealousy as Bryan told them that the group owned around 29 bars in Pattaya and were looking to expand into other parts of Thailand and even the surrounding countries.

'Bryan mate, you must be fucking loving this life!'

Although clearly chuffed with his current direction, Bryan just smiled and ordered a round of Fireballs for the entire bar.

Looking up at the logo adorning the horny hostesses tight uniform, Chilli downed his in doubled quick time and thought to himself

'Envy…they got that right!'

* * *

So It Begins...

Ice's head was pounding and she realised that she'd face a hefty laundry bill if she couldn't make it to the toilet in time. Three seconds later she recoiled as she could taste the rum on the vomit that was leaving her body far quicker than it had entered. Head spinning and sobbing with hunger pangs, she had never felt as pissed off as this morning. Or was it the afternoon already?

She seldom had a clue anymore. Her body clock was absolutely rotten, and all that she knew was, whatever time she woke up, she would be hungry and sweating like a stuck pig. So much for her knight in shining armour. What a prize tool he had turned out to be. She crawled back to her mattress and pulled the covers over her head. Fuck this life!

After their tacky embrace, the freelancer pulled Jack into the nearest bar and challenged him to a drinking game. It was fairly simple, just win a game of connect four, the loser has to down a shot in one, how hard could it be?

Bloody hard, so it turned out. Less than five games in and he was as pissed as he could ever remember.

'How much you pay me?'

She was direct, this one.

Her name was Noi and she was from some unpronounceable place upcountry. Nowhere near as pretty as Ice but still a mile better than any girl back home. He agreed on a fee of 2,000 baht - £50. Double the original quote but, for that price, she would do whatever he wanted and a few things besides. Having all but forgotten about Debs and given up on Ice, Jack decided that he may as well do what needed doing.

When they arrived back at his room in Soi 8, he was dismayed to see that Shaun was already in the room. It was now 4am and thankfully he was alone and looked as if he was flat out. Jack was less than happy having sex with Shaun in the room but Noi had no such reservations.

So It Begins...

She was already in the shower and was beckoning for him to jump in and join her. Jack didn't need to be asked twice and seconds later she was metaphorically scrubbing his back and other places that Debs never went anywhere near. If this was a typical night in Pattaya, he could certainly get used to it!

Noi had fallen on hard times recently and was fired from her last bar for stealing from the till. Bitch of a mamasan had been looking for a reason to fire her ever since Noi had been fucking her farang husband behind her back. She couldn't help it if the old man had preferred her firm boobs to some droopy spaniel ears.

Anyway, after that, no bar would take her on, as the previous boss knew many of the other mamasan's and had really put the boot in as far as her reputation was concerned. So, she had ended up working the street, quite literally, and it wasn't unusual for her to fuck five or six men a night. Sometimes she even went with married couples. That wasn't too bad so long as the farang lady had a shower and wasn't too fat or hairy.

This guy seemed a little nicer than the usual old perverts that gravitated towards Noi, but at the end of the day, they were all the same. Men were utter bastards.

Her own father had tried to rape her when she was less than ten years old. When Noi had told her mother, the old cow had sided with her husband and meted out a beating that Noi could still feel to this day. She was then farmed out to her grandparents and the day when her father came back for another go, Noi was ready for him. She was still only fourteen but worldly wise and when he produced his penis, she grabbed a pair of nearby shears and the flaccid organ was sliced off instantly. She left the village that night and never returned.

Working as an underage waitress in a Chiang Mai guesthouse was the entry point for a future in 'The Industry'. Fast forward twenty years and she was all but washed up at the grand old age of 35 years old.

So It Begins...

Her game plan these days was very simple but usually effective:
1. Meet someone on the Beach Road
2. Get them drunk as quickly as possible
3. Agree a price, although this wasn't the amount she would eventually get
4. Go back to the room
5. Shower
6. Have the customer shower
7. Have sex as quickly as possible
8. Wait for the customer to sleep
9. Look for more money in the room
10. Pour more booze down the customer's throat whilst they were sleeping
11. Wake them up
12. Demand money
13. Leave
14. Repeat

So far this had worked quite well but tonight there was a small problem, the bastard in the other bed! Not enough to put her off, Noi was a very crafty little whore and she would work out a game plan that would be more than a match for these young buffaloes.

Jack dried off and it felt like bloody hours before Noi came to join him. She was inspecting the room and soon found the minibar. He half expected her to grab a bottle of chilled water for the mind-blowing sex he was going to give to this lucky bitch but she came back with a wicked grin and a small bottle of Mekong Whisky. She took a tiny swig and jammed the bottle between his lips and seemed intent on emptying the whole fucking lot into his already half pissed body.

So It Begins...

Jack pulled away as a decent size glug hit the pillow.

'Daft fucking Cow'

Jack murmured and pulled her across his bed as her damp towel slipped away.

Her body was pretty good but he wondered how many miles of cock had been through this slapper? He decided she had room for a few more and it was well and truly on.

Noi slipped a condom onto him using nothing but her full red lips, this was a nice little touch. Within 10 seconds, the freelancer was riding him as if it were a photo finish at the Grand fucking National. He'd never experienced sex like this, with Debs it was more like straddling a Blackpool seaside donkey.

Jack could sense some movement from the other bed and when he looked sideways, he saw something that made him lose any sex drive he had going on. Shaun was sat up in the bed and was playing with himself whilst staring intently at the sordid scene next to him.

'For fuck's sake you dirty little cunt!'

Jack knew that Shaun enjoyed masturbation in public places so this shouldn't have come as such a surprise, but still…

Noi didn't give two hoots, she'd seen it all and was focussed on her task right now. Eventually Jack gave up caring and just laid back and thought of Man City as this bizarre event came to a climax, or double climax if the gross moans from the adjacent bed were anything to go by.

If Jack had looked over a little earlier, he'd have been even more furious. Shaun had discretely whipped out his phone and had captured twenty seconds of the fucking activity and sent it direct to his sister via Facebook chat. He sniggered as he went back to sleep. He'd always had an issue with Jack marrying Debs and now he had hammered the final nail into his coffin.

So It Begins...

Although she hadn't enjoyed sex for years, this customer was quite attractive so there were worse ways to earn money. He'd drank a fair amount so soon it would be time for her to rifle the hotel room. The other man was dead to the world and if he woke up, well it would be a challenge that this North-Eastern girl could rise to.

To be fair, it was like the Thai version of shooting fish in a barrel usually and she had more than enough money to send home, if she still had somewhere to call home. Her grandparents were long since dead according to an old friend from the village. Her dad had, by all accounts, become a monk after his precious manhood had been fed to the ducks. As for her mother, well any woman who would let a man rape her daughter wasn't a person who she ever wanted to know again.

The sex act was going on a bit longer than she liked and when she noticed the other man touching himself, she started to think that this was going to be a difficult night. Fortunately, it only lasted another few minutes and by then, the other farang wasn't moving.

She was on the home straight!

After a quick cuddle, the room was full of snoring and Noi slipped out of the bed and the ransacking began. She was an expert on where to find money and valuables and first she checked the pockets of the jeans strewn on the floor, that was good for a few thousand baht. After that she'd check the shirt pockets and finally go for the room safe. This was wide open and contained nothing, not even passports. She had a good haul, adding up to around 5,000 baht. If she was lucky, she'd find another sucker on the beach road and may even hit double figures.

Before leaving she poured a few more shots down the sleeping farang's throat and finally woke him up with a few hard slaps. He came to and looked as if he would hurl.

'I go now! Give me money farang!'

She chuckled as the man lurched out of the bed and almost immediately fell over into a heap.

She'd done a number on this idiot. He slowly regained his balance and looked in his jeans and then his shirt. She was half waiting for him to lose his shit and accuse her of stealing but instead, he asked her to wait and half stumbled towards the door mumbling something about travellers cheques.

'Fucking Hell!'

Jack exclaimed; he'd not felt this pissed since New Year's Eve as a fourteen-year-old. That night he had helped himself to more than a few of Dad's prized rhubarb wines and spent the whole of New Year's Day with his head down the toilet. This was on a par and then some.

He was sure that he had left some high value notes in both shirt and jeans pocket but they were gone. Head far too mangled to think of anything else, Jack made it to the reception desk and thankfully he remembered the combination to his safety deposit box. He'd listened to his parent's advice against keeping passports and traveller's cheques in the room safe.

Despite the woeful exchange rate, he was soon back at the room with enough money to pay this whore and send her back to where he found her. But when he knocked on the door, he could hear some sort of commotion going on. Twenty seconds later, she yanked the door open, grabbed the contents of his hand and was gone without even a peck on the cheek, rude bitch!

Jack crawled back into bed and was fast asleep before a sheepish looking Shaun emerged from one of the walk in wardrobes.

Shaun had to laugh at the farcical event that had developed a few minutes earlier. All he could remember was being rudely awoken form his slumber by a garlic and whisky breathed bitch who was trying to prise open his closed fist. He often went to sleep with his money in his hand, couldn't remember when that odd habit started. He soon came to his senses when the girl stopped trying to get his money and started dry humping him for all she was worth. Quite a lot by the way she was grinding into him. If he hadn't had a wank earlier, he would have shot his muck already. Issues with premature ejaculation had all but ruined his life and it was something he had to deal with. But after a minute or so, Shaun could feel like he was almost ready for round two.

But then someone started knocking on the door! The girl sat bolt upright and demanded in broken English that he go hide in the wardrobe. As he obeyed her command, she was still holding onto his fist. Faced with losing a few quid or a beating from whoever was at the door, the tight bastard almost whimpered as he let go of the notes and darted for freedom. He stayed as quiet as a church mouse for five minutes, and eventually the coward pushed the wardrobe door open and crawled back into his bed, wondering what the fuck that was all about?

* * *

Noi was giggling almost controllably as she told her friends details of the comedy event she had just orchestrated. She had made over ten thousand baht from those stupid fuckers and was even treating her two best friends to an early breakfast. They listened over and over again and eventually became bored of the way that Noi kept exaggerating what had happened.

After the free meal, the two friends sloped off back to the beach road for one last try whilst Noi went back to her tiny room to catch up on some sleep before her monthly visit to the clinic. That itch had gotten worse and it was time to see if the rash in her inner thigh was ever going to clear up.

* * *

Chilli had a unique perspective on life, basically if something didn't hold his attention for more than ten seconds, it wasn't worth bothering about. Raised in an orphanage, he had no family to care for him and most of the people he called friends, couldn't really give a toss. When the chance to come on this extended stag weekend came up, it didn't take long for Chilli to raise his hand. He'd always wanted to come to Thailand and it certainly wasn't for the waterfalls and temples. Chilli liked the seedier side of life, and so far, Pattaya was holding up its end of the bargain.

His appearance made him stand out from the other two men and had been a matter of conversation ever since he started school back in Wallingford. His complexion was darker than the average pasty white Wallingford local and his eyes definitely had an oriental look, this was enough for him to be shunned for many years during his childhood. In a town that was typical Middle England, back in the 1990's, if you weren't white, you were an outsider. Perhaps this contributed to his behaviour, maybe not, but Chilli gave the impression that he could not give one iota of a fuck, no matter where he happened to be.

Shaun had long since gone back to the hotel and Chilli was enjoying a cold beer as the sun was rising. He'd left Soi 6, or Soi Nightwish as it was sometimes called, and made his way to an area known as Soi LK Metro.

To be fair, he preferred it this way as the other two certainly weren't his cup of tea. Jack was okay but stuck in a relationship with that stupid cow Debs. Her brother, Shaun, was a bloody retard, and it was only because he had planned this trip that Chilli was even acknowledging him.

The girl he had taken from Envy was starting to lag now, she'd matched him beer for beer but eventually it had taken its toll on the poor thing. He had tried to convince her to nip over to the beach for a quick shag but she wasn't having any of it. This surprised Chilli, after all, she was a prostitute so why should she care? He had a lot to learn about Thailand, that much was for sure.

The bar fine system was a surprise. He'd paid the bill and half expected her to tag along but she kept repeating something that sounded like 'pay bar, pay bar'. He patiently explained that he'd already done that even left a hefty ten baht tip…

Eventually one of the girls with decent English managed to get through to him. 500 baht worse off, he was again surprised when she disappeared and came back wearing jeans and a lot less make up. He would have preferred for her to keep her miniskirt and boob tube for the rest of the session but that didn't happen.

In most beer bars around Pattaya, if you want to take a lady for the night, you will need to pay the bar 500 baht, sometimes less, sometimes more, the bar will keep most of this. Gogo bars are typically 1,000 baht for the 'bar fine' and that is usually the same whether you take her for a short time or the whole night. In fact, many customers take the girl for the night and after an hour or two in the bedroom, it's not unusual for them to make an excuse and leave. 30 minutes later, the same girl is back on the stage looking for her second punter of the night.

He grew bored of the one-way conversation and just for a laugh, Chilli decided to go to the toilet and instead of coming back, he had hopped over a wall and did a proper runner. He sniggered as he imagined the look on that poor whore's face as she realised her customer wasn't coming back tonight. He didn't even think about the large bar bill that he'd also left behind.

Ten minutes and a mile away, Chilli stumbled into a fairly run-down bar that was known as simply 'Time for You' He climbed the stairs to the first level as there was nobody downstairs. This level had a few ropey looking old girls and quite a weird shaped bar. There was a large recess by each stool and when he sat down, he noticed a small set of curtains at groin level. This was fucking odd…

He ordered a Singha beer and was taking a glug when he noticed some movement behind the set of curtains. A brown face appeared and a hand grabbed him by the genitals, slowly but surely. Another face appeared, this time at face level, the other side of the bar.

'Mister it is 1,000 baht. For that, you get two shots or 30 minutes'.

Chilli chuckled as he realised that he had walked into a blow job bar. Handing over the cash, Chilli sat back and enjoyed one of the best half hours of his dirty little life. Approximately 45 minutes later he staggered back to the hotel, drained of bodily fluids and was soon nice and snug in his bed.

He'd done well as the other two were sharing a twin room and Chilli was allowed the luxury of his own crib. He drifted off to sleep and was dreaming of a weird and wonderful place where he was living behind two huge curtains. He leant over and pulled one back only to see an erect member staring at him with a single pink eye.

This wasn't good. But before the inevitable happened, there was a massive commotion and his kip was rudely interrupted as it seemed that the hotel room door was going to be kicked in.

'Alright, fucking wait a minute!', Chilli grunted as he unlocked the door.

A couple large Thai men burst in and pinned him to the bed. Then two women entered and were shouting at him like a pair of bloody witches. As he focussed, Chilli recognised one as the whore he had left in the lurch and the other was that tasty older lady who was serving him just before he'd ran off.

'Fucking hell, stop shouting and I'll pay you your fucking money!'

They continued shouting and the larger of the men started slapping him around the face. This wasn't a good way to start his second day in Thailand. After ten minutes of this treatment, they eventually let him sit up and then told Chilli in no uncertain terms that he had to pay them now plus 5000 baht besides or he would get the kicking of his life.

So It Begins...

He really wanted to tell them to do one but Chilli was no fighter and even if he was, these two old boys looked like they wanted to rip his head off. So, he paid up and they eventually left him to try and get back into that obscure dream. He couldn't slip back into kip mode especially as his head was sore after those slaps. Eventually giving up, he noticed it was already 11am and he decided to see if the other shitheads were awake yet.

When Chilli managed to find the hotel restaurant, he could see that both of his travelling buddies were already there. But it appeared that he'd walked in on a bad situation. Usually on a stag weekend, no matter where the location, the morning meal would be full of boasting and bravado regarding the previous night's adventures and escapades. There would be naming and shaming with evidence, should it be required, captured on smartphones.

But this was something else.

Neither man was speaking and they both had faces on them that could sink a ship.

'Morning wankers!' No effect.

'What the fuck happened to you two?'

'Bust Johnny?'

'Ladyboy surprise?'

'Snapped yer Banjo?'

He was on form today, but none of his usual jibes were working.

Chilli thought 'fuck it' and started digging into his mountain of a breakfast buffet plate wondering why his jaw hurt so much. Then there were signs of life from Shaun. He pulled his chair back and started messing with his smartphone.

Jack decided to pipe up.

'Mate, don't tell me your sister has been on the fucking blower yet again?'

This amused Shaun and he continued playing with his phone until he found what he was looking for.

'This better be good'.

Chilli said with a mouth full of bacon and eggs.

'Oh, it's top drawer mate'

Shaun's voice took on a sinister tone as he placed the device in the middle of the table, looking for an attentive audience. All three men sat up in their seats and concentrated on the small screen. The quality was fairly poor but after a few seconds it was obvious that the subject matter consisted of two people in bed, having fairly one-sided sex.

Jack squinted to get a better look and then recoiled in horror as he realised this was a recording of him fucking the freelancer eight or nine hours earlier. He was going to question his roommate when he noticed that the video was being played back from Facebook.

'Shaun, what the actual fuck is this?'

Even Chilli was speechless but not for long.

'Jack you dirty dog, she's riding you like Willie Carson in the Grand National'. He wasn't wrong.

'Yeah Jack, if you're wondering if Debs knows, she's seen it 40 times already mate'

'Morning boys, ready for the beach?'

Frank had interrupted what was sure to be a real shitstorm.

Chilli had bumped into him just before his first visit upstairs in Envy and he'd offered to show him and the others Pattaya in the daytime.

Realising that things were going to kick off between Jack and Shaun, Chilli ushered the older man away and they moved towards the hotel bar.

So It Begins...

Despite the slight distraction, Jack was seething and he flew across the table dragging Shaun to the floor. Pinning him to the ground, he rained at least a dozen punches into Shaun's face before standing up. Shaun, although in some pain, still had that shit eating grin on his bloody face.

'Get your stuff out of my room you two faced little cunt!'

As Shaun tried to get up, Jack kicked him so hard up the arse that he fell forward and was sprawled on the floor like a huge starfish.

Laughing like a deranged idiot, Shaun wiped some blood from his mouth and walked out of the restaurant, aware that dozens of eyes were following his every step.

Jack tried to leave the scene of the battle but Chilli managed to grab his arm just before he reached the door.

'Fucking hell boy, you gave him a right kicking, although the cunt totally deserved it. I never like that sneaky shit anyway'.

Jack couldn't really hear these comments but was in a state of disarray as Chilli shared his plans of hitting the beach in a few hours.

When he got back to his room, he saw that Shaun had done the decent thing and cleared his stuff out. Lying down on his bed, Jack was full of confusion and regrets but they weren't for Debs, nor were they anything to do with the slapping he'd just meted on Shaun.

No.

His only regrets were that he wasn't even remotely sure where the girl from last night was. Ice…

End of Chapter One

▲ The infamous Soi 6 – Photo by Fernando

Chapter Two
THE MORNING AFTER

They say that time heals all wounds, and this may be true because Jack had grabbed a few hours' sleep and when he woke up, things seemed a lot clearer. He got the fact that he never had real feelings for Debs, for if he had, they would be in Benidorm right now and in bed together.

Instead, he was in Thailand and now his mind was starting to focus on the girl from last night. He'd fucked things up royally with her, but he was here for three more days, so why shouldn't he try and find her again?

Shaun had done his worst and although things would be crap back at home, here he was, youngish, free and definitely single.

There was a knock on the door and before he could stand up, Chilli marched in and started spouting shit about going to the beach.

'We're going to the beach Young Man! Maybe we can find that chick you are moping over. Not the trollop on Facebook but that pretty little thing from the first bar'.

Jack wasn't remotely interested until Chilli revealed his trump card: 'So I spoke with some girls just now and they said that she lives near the beach...'

Jack looked up and pushed him towards the door and grinned.

'I'll be down in ten minutes'.

Chilli chuckled to himself as he trotted downstairs where Frank was waiting.

'Gullible fuck', He muttered under his breath as he ordered a beer.

* * *

In fact, Ice didn't live anywhere near the beach but she was still missing him and had started to make up excuses for his bad behaviour the previous night.

'Why you care that farang?' her best friend Nok asked her as she tapped furiously into her iPhone.

'He's just another customer, and you are still pretty enough to get a man any time you need money'.

Nok was hardcore and she'd been in Pattaya for nearly ten years.

She had taken Ice under her wing and despite her hard exterior, underneath beat a heart of pure Thai gold.

'Please can you help me find him? I worry he will find another lady now'.

Nok scoffed at her soft friend but had a feeling that she wouldn't get any peace as Ice was the most stubborn person she'd ever met.

'You pay me 100 baht and I can find this one for you, but you pay me now okay?'

Ice handed over the red note and started massaging her friend's shoulders as if this would speed her up in this romantic manhunt. To be fair, if anyone could track a person down on Facebook, it was Nok. After confirming his full name, which was discovered after a few calls to the hotel opposite the bar where they met, the search was on.

Pattaya is a place that is built on networking and the chances are if a Thai person doesn't know someone who works in a particular hotel, they will know someone else who does.

Jack isn't a rare name but his surname helped to narrow down that demographic nicely. According to Facebook, there were four Jack Roberts who lived in England.

One of them looked 80, two didn't have a profile picture and the 4th one, well he looked a lot like Ice's target. Once this was confirmed, they sent a friend request and went out for some lunch as the bait was laid.

* * *

'So Frank, how long are you in Pattaya for?

The older man smiled and replied, 'I'm here until New Year mate!'

Even Jack snapped out of his disinterested mood and both younger men waited for Frank to continue.

'Lads, I've got fuck all back home, wife left me 10 years ago, and my kids, well they only want to know me when they need something. So when my work dried up, I thought it was time to look after number one'.

He explained that he was laid off and was given one month's salary for each year.

That added up to just over 30 grand.

Even Chilli was impressed.

As the three men boarded the baht bus taxi to Jomtien beach, he started firing questions at Frank, as if it were an interview.

'How much Thai money is that?'

'At today's shit exchange rate, it's just over 1.2 Million baht'

'Will that last you?'

'Well, as I'm a hansum man, I should fucking well hope so!'

Chilli and Jack giggled at this description, they'd both already heard it many times.

'Anyway lads, who's the jet-ski bloke?'

Chilli took a deep breath and took his time explaining to Frank that there was a bit of a gangster back in Wallingford who did business with a Thai man called Sparky. He was a proper wheeler and dealer and Johnny had told Chilli to look him up if he wanted anything dodgy in Pattaya. Jet-skis may not be that big of a deal but there were plenty of scams going on in Pattaya with this line of business. Frank already had his reservations but stayed quiet.

'What the actual fuck!'

Chilli blurted out as they took a corner and the taxi was forced to slam on its brakes. There, right in the middle of the road was a sight none of them would ever forget.

Three bare chested men were attempting to cross the busy road. The two on the outside were doing their level best to help the poor man in between them. But the men in the taxi weren't looking at him, they were all focussed on the five meter long piece of wood that was sticking out of his head.

'We ain't in Kansas anymore Toto'

Chilli giggled and found it hard to suppress his mirth as Jack just looked in absolute shock.

The taxi allowed them to cross and as they pulled past the three Thai men, one of them smiled and looked directly at them and said one word:

'Accident…'

The poor blighter with half a tree in his head even smiled at them as he wobbled along. This was just one example of how Thai people seem to just deal with tragedy and accept whatever fate is around the corner.

Pattaya is one of those places where the rule book has long since been torn to pieces and fed to a hungry stray dog.

The taxi then passed through South Pattaya which was already a hive of activity.

'Hey lads, just look at the tits on him!'

The Morning After

Chilli was in high spirits as he pointed out a large breasted Ladyboy who had clearly decided to wear a bra that was two or three sizes too small for him/her.

Jack shook his head and tutted. Chilli was a proper little piss taker and he wondered if the reason for his orphan status had been because his parents had been able to see into the future and had decided to cut their losses.

After an uneventful five minutes, most of it spent travelling up a large bendy steep road, the taxi pulled into a layby and they hopped out of the back and surveyed the scene ahead. Okay so it wasn't exactly paradise, but for now, Jomtien Beach was pretty damn close. Lined with coconut trees and some fairly decent white sand, it looked incredible.

* * *

Meanwhile Shaun was sat in a nondescript bar nursing his jaw, he didn't think Jack had it in him but that was some kicking. He chuckled as he imagined the absolute shit storm that he had created this morning. Sure, Debs would be broken hearted for a while but he had done her a real favour. Jack was only sniffing round her because he had nowhere to live, and Debs, bless her heart, well, she was no Scarlett Johansson.

Although he and Jack were once tight, they had drifted apart and Shaun had never forgiven him for 'stealing' the woman he loved.

Truth told, he had only seen her for the first time at midnight in the Didcot disco but by 2am, Jack was getting a blow job from her in the train station disabled toilets.

Even though the fling didn't last longer than the next football season, Shaun had never even got close to finding another girl he had fancied.

As for Debs, well she was a randy old slapper who had fucked most of his mates before they hit puberty, all except Jack.

Once Jack had shown her the slightest interest, she was smitten. Dozy fucking cow!

There were three more days left so he was damned if he was going to spend the rest of that time sulking. Shaun decided to check out of that crappy hotel and find somewhere a little classier. He punched in a few search parameters into his smartphone and was amazed to discover that there was a four-star place around the corner. He saw a few text messages from that idiot Chilli, something to do with a beach and jet-skis. Not even remotely interested, Shaun grabbed his suitcase and started walking towards the South end of Pattaya City.

* * *

After spending a small fortune on street food, Ice was stuffed with noodles and chicken and had to admit that Nok was a one off. Ice pulled the device out of her hand and started looking at his profile. There wasn't much to see but she almost dropped it when she noticed that his status read 'engaged'. Although her English was fairly crap, even she knew that this meant one thing – he was not single.

Why should she care? After all, she was a bar girl and the luxury of morals and standards weren't something that usually mattered to this demographic. But Ice was different. Her heart sank as she handed the battered Samsung back to Nok. But her friend was having none of this.

'You stupid bitch', She shrieked.

'If he was in love with a girl in his country, why the fuck is he here?'

This made some sense, after all, he didn't exactly pull away when she was rubbing his crotch. Maybe he was worth another shot?

Ice's phone vibrated and her face lit up like a Christmas tree.

'He accepts the friend request!'

Nok sneered and chided her friend,

The Morning After

'Haha, your face, it's like someone one the lottery, you are so soft!'

But Ice didn't care, all she wanted now was to find Jack. But how? Maybe her Social Media specialist could help her even more?

Nok sensed this and before Ice could open her mouth, she held out her mitt and said three words:

'500 baht!'

They shook hands and the White Buffalo hunt was well and truly on…

Earlier, Shaun had checked into the Penthouse Hotel and had paid a little extra for the Junior Suite. It had a massive bed and a balcony and a minibar. But the main attraction was the elevated hot tub.

He turned on the TV and was surprised to see that one channel was dedicated to the go-go bar in the basement. It wasn't open yet but you could use the interactive app to pick the dancer that tickled your fancy the most. The receptionist downstairs had explained that they would be up and, in your room, before you could sing the British National Anthem! This was more like it!

But he'd also seen a few interesting bars on the way to the hotel. Pretty low key and a bit more earthy than the ones he'd staggered around the night before. After a cheeky beer on the balcony, he sprayed some Brut 33 on his nuts and under his arms and was ready to hit the scene.

* * *

As soon as Chilli heard the Jet-ski engines firing up, he knew he had to be the first one to have a go. It had always been this way. Since his orphanage days, he had tried his best to be the first in the queue, regardless of what was on offer. But he absolutely loved speed and these devices looked like something he would be good at. Back in Wallingford he had been banned for three years for reckless driving and this had been a real pisser. But before he could show Jack how good he was, they had to speak to some Thai lad that ran the business.

Sparky looked up and groaned inwardly when he saw the three farangs walking towards them. Their feet were being burnt by the hot sand and even this comical sight failed to raise a grin. Why the fuck did the man back in the UK keep sending these morons to his beach? Okay, they weren't too bad for business, but he would prefer to get those Indian or Japanese tourists that were easier to scam.

He made a small fortune from the legitimate trade but that was a drop in the ocean compared to the millions of baht he amassed from ripping off the clueless rich idiots that made the mistake of hiring his jet-skis. The scam was nothing new, still, it did the job pretty well.

Here's how it worked:
1. Find a perfectly good jet-ski
2. Scratch a sizeable portion of the white hull with an abrasive material, ensure this is not visible above the water line
3. Paint over this with a substance that dissolves after being in salt water for more than 20 minutes
4. Find a gullible foreign tourist, Chinese and Indians are the easiest.
5. Rent the jet-ski out for 30 minutes or more
6. Do a physical examination and ask them to sign a form stating that there is no physical damage.
7. When the jet-ski is returned, do a physical examination and point out the damage to the hull whilst calling over a few intimidating colleagues.
8. Explain that to repair this damage will cost in excess of 50k baht but allow them to plea down to 25,000
9. Should they kick up a fuss, call in the Tourist Police who will take a small fee for their 'help'

The Morning After

This little plan had worked for years and had allowed Sparky to build up a large empire of jet-skis, speedboats, bars, and more than a dozen minor wives.

So today was pretty slow as far as business was concerned and these deadbeats may well prove to be decent bait for easier prey. He fixed a fake smile and went over with his hand outstretched…

Jack was enjoying the lovely Thai weather and, although he couldn't get that excited about the boys' day out on the beach, he was smiling inwardly. In fact, he was pretty stoked. Since the friend request from Ice had popped up on his screen, he could think of nothing else but holding her soft body close to his.

'Jack, you soppy git, come down and have a go on these things!'

He looked up and could see that Chilli, typically, was already out there and was imitating Barry Sheen as he zipped across the choppy sea. Right now, all he was concentrating on now was connecting with this girl and moving on, away from the miserable present and past.

Sparky had introduced himself to the group and, because of the connection with his contact back in Wallingford, there would be no scams with this bunch. After five minutes, a few Chinese tourists started to arrive. 'Hello Mistah! You want Jet-ski?', He bellowed out towards them as a few of his sidekicks started handing out fliers to the unsuspecting suckers.

* * *

'Okay sister, we go now'.

Nok held out her hand for the 500 baht and Ice paid her without flinching.

'But how have you found him, and so fast?'

Nok held her finger up to her lips as if it was the world's biggest secret and skipped towards the door. It had been simple, this time there was no digital shenanigans. A simple phone call to her cousin who worked for the Pattaya Taxi firm had been enough to track the target down.

'We go Jomtien!'

Nok shouted above the motorbike revs as Ice kicked it into life.

She had put on her best lipstick and the shortest dress because this was an entrance she wanted Jack to remember forever, or at least for a few hours.

* * *

Chilli was having the time of his life; he couldn't believe that he'd never been on a jet-ski. There weren't many places in Oxfordshire where he could have a blast like this but he was sure that he'd find somewhere when he got back. He pulled the throttle back and gunned the thing directly at poor old Frank and squealed with laughter as he could see the terror in his eyes as he did everything he could to avoid a collision.

He didn't really care if he hit him or not, it was worth it for the crack. Anyway, how much would these Thai wankers want for a crashed jet-ski? Besides which, he would tell them to do one if they got funny. It was as if the beating he had received less than twelve hours ago didn't really happen. The lads back at home were proper football hooligans and just because Sparky knew them, that didn't really bother Chilli. He'd got by on bravado and bottle so far and that hadn't let him down.

By contrast, Sparky was not a happy man.

Firstly, the Chinese tourists hadn't rented his jet-skis and now, well now this English bastard was hell bent on crashing his best machine. Despite the furious waves and shouting from the beach, the idiot kept aiming his craft directly at anything in his path. Chilli was riding hands-free, enjoying the danger.

He looked around for the other member of this pathetic posse and could see that he was chatting to two sexy looking Thai women that had just pulled up on a motorbike. Maybe he was the only sensible one in the group?

Suddenly, he heard someone scream 'Look Out!' and then a loud bang from the bay and swivelled around to see that the idiot had driven the jet-ski straight into a large crop of rocks. The crap day had become even worse than he could have imagined.

Jomtien beach wasn't that large and within two or three minutes of turning onto the strip, Nok and Ice had found their quarry. Nok parked the bike as close to the farang as was possible but Ice had already jumped off the back and was waving at the man she was infatuated with. At least he seemed pleasantly surprised as well. She couldn't stand the ones who thought they were actually worth the effort. Nok had long since given up any hope of meeting one that held her interest so she looked on with a distant curiosity as the two lovebirds approached each other.

As far as Jack was concerned, this was something straight out of a Mills and Boon as Ice ran towards him across the beach. All that was missing was some cheesy music and a slow motion visual. She seemed delighted and as they hugged and kissed, he had never felt this elated. After what felt like minutes, she gently pulled back and stared into his eyes. Fucking hell, she was actually crying now, hopefully tears of joy.

He was no romantic, but Jack wished he could simply stop the clock and just drink her in, drop by drop.

Ice was just going to say something when a huge bang from the sea wrecked that near perfect moment. Jack looked around and his heart sank as he realised that Chilli had pranged the bloody jet-ski into a large rock. Chilli went flying off the vehicle into the water, and the whole beach was transformed as Sparky and his men jumped onto their jet-skis to the crime scene. At least half a dozen Thai men zipped across the waves to the accident spot. Jack was surprised at their speed and even more so when two of them dived off in unison and started beating the life out of Chilli.

So much for safety first, thought Jack and he made his excuses to Ice and her lovely friend in order to get to Chilli while he was still breathing. The two Thai men dragged him through the shallow water and the beating continued until Sparky had ordered them to stop.

Frank had tried to intervene but was clever enough not to get aggressive. In his years of travelling to Thailand he knew that you would be fairly safe unless you got involved in a fight, especially when the numbers are stacked against you.

Chilli was lucky that he had friends that had some influence, otherwise this little motherfucker would already be fish food. That jet-ski was almost brand new and cost half a million baht. What's more, it had the earning potential of at least twice that over twelve months. Sparky ordered his thugs to drop Chilli, and as he hit the soft sand, he gave out a whimper that sounded more like a spurned street dog than a human. He was okay really, just a few cuts and bruises, and lungs full of salt water. The remainder of the crew were doing their best to bring the smashed craft back onto the beach before it sank.

Jack was torn because although he wanted to be there for his friend, he really needed to get back to Ice to finally seal this deal. She was back at the motorbike with her friend, it was as if they knew some shit was going to go down and were keeping their distance.

'What happened?'

Chilli murmured, he didn't look so fucking smug now, thought Sparky. He walked away and started phoning an overseas number. He needed to know who Chilli was and how well connected he might be. Thais had a strong belief in the Face system but Sparky also knew what side his bread was buttered on. The man in Wallingford put a lot of business his way and he returned the favour. The call was answered and two or three minutes later, he hung up and walked back towards the group.

He cast a gaze towards the two girls, they both looked good enough to eat, maybe today wasn't such a shit one after all.

Are you Jack?' Sparky demanded.

Jack looked up and nodded.

I need to speak to you; Johnny from Wallingford says you are the only one here with half a brain'.

Sparky sniggered as he repeated that phrase, it tickled him and he'd use it again one day, probably.

Johnny was the top boy back home and he ran things. Football Hooligan was too crude a term for this man. He had his finger in many pies and wasn't to be messed with.

Jack and Sparky walked for twenty metres and when the Thai man placed his hand on his shoulder, he stopped to face him.

'Jack, your friend has made a fucking big problem'.

That was pretty obvious.

'I spoke to Johnny who told me that Chilli has no money and no friends back home'

Bit harsh, but on the money.

'But, he also said that he likes you and to give your mate a chance'.

Jack noticed that Sparky kept looking to the left where the two girls were standing. He also shot them a gaze and both were now looking awkwardly at their feet, as if they were facing detention at school.

'How much money does Chilli have?'

Sparky's voice had turned very serious and it was if he was looking directly into Jack's soul. He was going to reply when Sparky continued.

'I need half a million baht for the damage'

Jack's internal calculator started doing the maths. The exchange rate was currently 40 Thai Baht to the pound.

'That's more than twelve grand,'

Jack was thinking out loud.

'Otherwise, he is fucked…'

He said these words almost the same second as Jack's brain finally reached that sum.

Jack still hadn't replied and when he looked up the Thai man was already walking back, still leering at Ice and her friend.

Half an hour later Jack and Frank were stood around a bed at Pattaya Hospital looking down on a dejected and, for once, quiet Chilli. Nok and Ice were outside, and this was more than they had bargained for. His face had taken a beating, the second one in 24 hours, and although not a great looker, he now resembled Elephant Man.

'You absolute fucking twat!'

Jack was fuming and let loose on Chilli for a good two or three minutes.

'Have you any idea how much shit you are in mate?'

He went on to explain that Chilli needed to come up with twelve and a half big ones in the next two days.

Chilli half smirked as he replied.

'Twelve and a half Grand, I haven't got twelve and a half fucking pence…'

He'd funded this trip on his credit card and now that was maxed to the limit. There was nobody back in Wallingford that liked him enough to help.

'I have £500 back at the hotel but was hoping to spend that on whores and booze, the rest I'd waste…'

His feeble attempt at a joke failed to hit the spot.

Frank motioned for Jack to step outside the ward for a chat.

'Listen my friend, this is a serious situation, do you understand?'

'Thai people are the nicest and most gentle on earth, but when you mess with their income, in a public show like today, they will kill you. I've never had a problem here, but your friend, well, I'm surprised that you are hanging around with someone so reckless'.

Both men were sitting down when Frank offered Jack a possible solution.

'I can lend you some money, not the whole amount, but enough to keep the wolves at bay'.

Jack was astonished, they'd only met Frank a handful of times and he was prepared to hand over a substantial amount of cash. Placing his hand firmly on Frank's shoulder, Jack looked him straight in the eyes and replied,

'Frank, that is so fucking generous of you and I would like nothing better than to accept your offer'.

He went on as Frank listened intently.

'But I can't pay you back and that little twat certainly won't, even if he could.'

'I understand, but remember, the offer is good'.

Both men walked back into the ward to see Chilli smiling like an idiot. He'd been listening to the conversation, another of his annoying traits.

'Fuck you Jack, Frank I'll take your offer!'

Jack just shook his head and Frank, caught in two minds, announced that he was going to check out a new bar he had heard about.

Jack was trying to think of another solution to this nightmare but his mind kept wandering.

'Ah bollocks, I'm going to go and take Ice back to my room and will be back in the morning'.

'Oooh check you out with your little whore girlfriend... Does she charge you, or is it on the house?'

Chilli was still being a little shit, despite having the stuffing knocked out of him.

That was the end of this conversation as far as Jack was concerned and he walked out of the hospital ward to find Ice waiting alone outside. He had less than 48 hours left in Pattaya and finally he could start enjoying it.

* * *

Even though Thai women were pretty enough, Shaun wasn't overly impressed so far. He preferred taller girls, with bigger tits. The ones he'd groped so far had fried eggs at best and their arses were too small and petite. He liked a bit of meat to bite into.

That was the reason he did a proper double take when he first spotted Mimi. Shaun fancied a go on her straight away, but she wasn't quite as taken. This was another attribute that piqued his interest. There was a challenge on offer and that was enough to make up his mind. He'd have her and make her beg for more. He wasn't the least bit romantic but Shaun had a massive ego that needed feeding right now.

He felt aggrieved that Chilli hadn't backed him up earlier and was going to get a bollocking from Debs when he returned in a few days' time. So why the fuck shouldn't he at least make it worthwhile? Mimi certainly ticked all of the physical boxes and when she reluctantly accepted a beer, Shaun started to feel almost human again.

* * *

Ice was a little shaken by the Jomtien beach scene but that wasn't enough to put her off the chase. Once they'd left the hospital, she and Jack headed back to his hotel and she could sense that he wanted this as much as she did, if that was possible. They were just passing the reception and towards the elevator when the old lady behind the desk held out her hand with a stern look on her face.

'ID card please'.

Her heart sank a little as this had almost shattered the mood, but not quite. Before Jack could say anything, she produced the document and put her finger to his lips.

He didn't know the way that hotels worked in Pattaya. Basically, they would treat any single Thai woman as a prostitute, even if they were not. But in this case, well, they were 100% right.

Two minutes later, they were in the air-conditioned room and Jack tore off his shirt as she kicked off her trainers. Usually she would insist that a customer took a shower but right now she wanted him inside her like she had never wanted anyone before. He pulled Ice onto the bed and they started kissing like a couple of teenagers. This was another new feeling for her. He tasted good and smelt even better.

As he entered her, Ice started to tremble and she began to ride this wonderful man as if she'd just discovered sex for the very first time.

Jack had never been that much of a lover but the last 15 minutes had certainly made him feel like a fucking stallion.

They both collapsed on the bed breathless as she started to giggle uncontrollably. He looked down and was surprised to see a used condom by his side, he'd not even noticed her slip it on in the heat of the moment. He started to wonder how many times she had done this before but as she climbed on top of him for a second time with a new condom between her teeth, it really didn't fucking matter…

They spent the next twelve hours in bed and lost count of how many times they made love.

She disappeared for fifteen minutes and returned with a bag full of exotic Thai fruits for them to munch on. Her favourite was the fragrant Chompoo, a red deciduous fruit also known as the rose apple. Chilli, Shaun, Debs, and even Sparky didn't exist within this special moment in time. That could all be dealt with tomorrow, or at least Jack hoped that was the case.

Ice was absolutely knackered; she had never come so much in her life, and never with a Westerner. She slipped into a series of dreams and Jack featured in them heavily. Mainly, they were together, and the very best one was where they were in a building that Ice presumed was a Western Church. She'd seen enough Rom Coms to know what weddings look like, and as they walked back down the aisle, bridesmaids in tow. She never wanted that feeling to end.

They woke with a start as a series of loud knocks were raining down on the hotel room door.

'Open now!'

Jack got out of the bed and looked back at Ice before opening the door slowly.

Sparky had a face like thunder and it was obvious that something bad had happened. Chilli had done a runner from his hospital bed. This had changed things dramatically, because Sparky was obviously not a man to mess with.

'That little fucking shit!'

Sparky didn't respond, he just motioned for Jack to follow him.

Kissing Ice on the cheek, Jack went with him to the Hospital.

Hoping against hope that the idiot had come to his senses and returned, he visibly groaned when they realised his bed had already been given to a more deserving patient. Chilli had absconded during the night and not one soul had any recollection of him leaving the building. Jack tried calling Shaun as it appeared that a temporary truce was needed, but he failed to answer.

Sparky beckoned for Jack to follow him into a side room. None of the doctors on the ward made eye contact with Sparky, Jack noted, it was as if they knew he was bad news.

'Okay Jack, now we have a bigger problem'.

Before he could reply, Sparky held his finger to his lips as Ice had earlier. Must be a Thai thing.

'Now there are two, maybe three choices for you'.

'Jesus fucking Christ', Jack thought, some stag weekend this was turning out to be. Not only did he discover that he didn't love his fiancée, now his buddy had got him tied up with mafia gangsters who were threatening his life. He didn't see what this had to do with him personally, and he knew that Chilli wouldn't so much as piss on him if he was on fire. So why did he have to deal with this at all?

'Okay, what are my choices?' He decided to play along for a while.

Sparky was relishing his role here.

'Your first choice is that you pay me the half million baht'.

No fucking chance of that.

'Second choice, we find your friend and kill him, slowly'.

Again, Sparky was grinning as if this was his personal preference.

'And choice three?' Jack was genuinely curious here, how bad could choice three be?

'You pay me half the money, I fuck your girlfriends for a whole week, and I put your other friend in hospital, for more than one week'. He cackled and Jack realised this was actually Sparky's top trump.

'How long do I have before I choose?'

Sparky's face was now consumed with hatred and he spat out the words with pure disgust.

'You choose now, fucking farang, you choose now!'

End of Chapter Two

▲ *Phone wins every time – Photo by Paul Eddie Yates Photography*

Chapter Three
REALITY BITES

Walking back to the hotel, Jack was cursing his luck. He'd travelled halfway around the world to be set up by his ex-buddy Shaun, met the love of his life and now Chilli was missing. He had less than two days left here in Pattaya and was properly torn between spending that time with Ice or trying to find Chilli.

Ice had just enjoyed the most tender night of sex that she'd ever imagined and, true to form, the man had all but disappeared. Maybe he had been playing her? Not really true as it was her and her intrepid sidekick had done all of the running. So, where was he? She checked her phone and it was now just after midday. Jack had been gone for two hours. She had tried calling him but there was no reply. She was worried that Sparky may have done something to Jack. Another reason she hated Thai men was that they had zero respect for anyone except themselves. Spoilt by their mothers as soon as they were born, they usually ended up causing a shitload of trouble for the family until they day they dropped dead, usually as drunks or druggies.

Ice found it inexplicable that a white buffalo could be her Prince Charming. She hadn't had good sex for far too long and had concluded that being a prostitute meant that no man would make her feel special enough that she could let her guard down and succumb to the emotions she needed to reach an orgasm. Being paid for sex meant that she was just a piece of meat, not human. This man treated her like she was royalty, and her body responded in kind.

She took a shower and couldn't resist running her fingers over her nipples as she played back her retrospective climaxes, one by one. She felt moisture between her legs, and it wasn't from the shower spray. Then just before orgasm number four came into play, the bathroom door opened and there he was!

Jack had jogged all the way from the hospital and was dripping wet by the time he got back to the hotel. His head was spinning, and he literally had no idea what he was going to do next. Ice's beautiful face certainly helped him to come to terms with the choice he had made.

There was no way he was going to be able to find Twelve odd grand, especially now the Bank of Debs was well out of the picture. He also couldn't put Ice and her friend through the undoubtable torture they'd be bound to experience at the hands of Sparky and most of his crew.

Option three, well Chilli was a proper fuck nugget, but did he deserve to die?

Before he could answer that one, a slender arm reached out of the steaming shower cubicle and he was, thankfully, dragged away from this hideous set of choices, if only for a little while.

The next day and a half literally flew by for Jack and Ice as they alternated between bed and shower and occasionally surfaced for food and liquids. So, when the time came to return to the UK reared its ugly head, they both started to realise that they needed to deal with the stark reality.

For Jack it was the tedium of a semi-existence back in Wallingford with no lucrative employment prospects, and the certain showdown with his ex-fiancé to look forward to.

For Ice, well her future may not have been as boring as her lover's but it was certainly far riskier and fuller of potential danger. She'd have to deal with this on her own, and without the slightest indication that Jack was feeling the same way, who knows what future, if any, they had together? Would he want to develop a romantic relationship knowing that she was servicing random customers day and night? As far as she knew, he'd be running home to the loving arms of his fiancée, bragging all the while to his mates about the epic stag weekend.

Okay, she could count the number of bargirls who ended up happily married, on the fingers of her left hand. There were literally hundreds who fell by the wayside and ended up lining the beach road waiting to turn tricks with whoever might show an interest. Right now, after this lovely experience, she wasn't even sure if she had the strength to do that.

'Jack, will you come back for me?'

They were munching through a bag of rose apples when Ice asked this question.

'Absolutely I will!'

He'd been wondering that very same thing and was trying for the life of him how to ensure that this wasn't just an empty promise.

'It will be a while though'.

She understood and didn't press the matter, there was no point in wasting their last few hours together.

'Ice, is it okay if we say goodbye here, and not at the airport?'

He looked longingly into her eyes and could see the pain that was staring back at him.

'Why?'

Jack did his level best to explain that he was worried for Sparky and Chilli and he hoped that his friend would somehow make an appearance.

'Okay, I understand, but you not fool me okay?'

Jack didn't like that term, too American but, he totally got what Ice was saying.

'No fooling, I will keep my promise. I will come back to you'.

That was the last they spoke of the next step and after the room service had dished up a huge bowl of Tom Yam Goong, they showered together for the last time and devoured each other as if it was their last ever act on this earth.

Jack kissed his lover goodbye outside the hotel and he'd already paid her most of his remaining cash back in the room. Ice had told him that she would travel back to Buriram and wait for him there, but he needed to send some money every month. He agreed but had no fucking idea how he would keep that promise.

Frank was just appearing as the taxi arrived and he gave Jack a firm handshake.

'Mate, I will keep an eye out for young Chilli and let you know if he shows up'.

Jack squeezed back and replied

'Cheers Frank, you are a good bloke, but please stay away from Sparky and his people, it's not your problem'.

Frank winked and Jack climbed into the taxi with a heavy heart.

* * *

At the airport, checking in his bags, he noticed Shaun arriving with a tall companion in tow. Quite striking but very obviously a ladyboy, Jack smiled inwardly as he watched the spectacle approach. The exaggerated movements and baritone voice were even more noticeable in the formal setting of the airport, and for a few seconds at least, the thought of Chilli and his uncertain future were forgotten.

'Alright Jack, where's Chilli then?'

Shaun asked before giving his companion a huge kiss and hugged her goodbye.

Silence.

'You see, Johnny was in touch and was pretty keen on him staying behind'.

Jack shook his head.

'You fucking twat Shaun, not only have you singlehandedly screwed up your sister's wedding, but now you are ready to throw Chilli to the wolves?'

'For starters, I did Debs a favour, you piece of shit, and secondly, who the actual gives a fuck what happens to Chilli anyway?' Shaun chuckled.

Shaun checked his bags in and walked away without looking back. Jack eventually followed but noticed that a few dodgy looking Thai men were hanging around without even trying to blend in. The fact that these men were there told him that Chilli was still very much at large.

Having a lightbulb moment, he decided to call Chilli's mobile. Without any real hope of an answer, he was amazed when his mate suddenly picked up.

'Jack, is that you?'

Looking around just in case those goons were close by, he carried on walking and listened to his desperate sounding friend.

'I'm in the toilets, opposite the security gates'.

Jack remained silent but his heart was beating ten to the dozen. Chilli was a slippery fucker, and somehow he'd managed to get to the airport without being caught.

Looking ahead, he spotted the sign for the toilets and decided he needed to take a piss right away.

The toilet was huge, even by airport standards. As he started to urinate, Jack heard what sounded like a man trying very hard to not to be found.

There were twelve cubicles to check and by the time he'd worked his way through half of them, the main door opened again and Jack groaned as he saw the two heavy set Thai men with a smug looking Shaun just behind them. They both produced sidearms and pointed them directly at

Jack's head indicating for him to get out. As he walked past Shaun they exchanged looks and Jack had never felt so much hatred in his whole life.

Twenty seconds later the door opened again and this time they appeared dragging an unconscious man.

It was Chilli.

Shaun sauntered past Jack and this time he was looking at the ground. Possibly just coming to terms with the fact he'd sentenced Chilli to death, or even worse.

Jack thought about alerting the airport police but by the time he'd found a lone security guard, Chilli and his captors had long gone. He tried to have a look outside but it was no use, there were hundreds of people arriving and leaving the airport. After 25 minutes, Jack had given up and started walking back to the immigration gate when he heard an announcement over the tannoy system.

'Last call for flight TG916 to London'

Christ, he'd almost missed the fucking plane.

Ten minutes later, as Jack took his seat on the long flight back home, he was feeling very low and very angry. Shaun had managed to find a seat away from him and this was a good thing. He would keep for now. He hadn't even had time to think of Ice, there would be plenty of time for that later.

Less than twelve hours later the plane landed at Heathrow airport and within minutes of disembarking, the cold air made him shiver involuntarily as he wearily prepared for a whole new set of problems.

After passing through the ball ache that was UK passport control, Jack walked to the baggage collection carousel. Shaun was already there and had lost much of his bravado, maybe he was feeling a little guilty, thought Jack. How wrong could someone be?

What would he do for his missing friend? Despite the sad fact that Chilli had nobody waiting for him at home, not even a distant relative, the authorities needed to be informed. He had no clue if the poor bastard was even alive.

As Jack pulled his suitcase off the carousel and onto the trolley, he noticed that Shaun was hanging back just before the customs area. Perhaps he wanted a chat or, more likely, he wanted to gloat.

'Listen mate, what happens next is totally on you'. Shaun spat the words out and the vitriol returned to his body language.

What the fuck was he on? Thought Jack, as he swerved around the smug twat.

The customs officials were as disinterested as they could possibly be and as Jack pushed his trolley around the corner, he could hear a strange yet familiar noise.

Behind him Shaun yelled out.

'HEY EVERYBODY - ATTENTION! Here he is; presenting the newest Internet sensation, Jack the Sex Pest Cheating shitbag!'

'Who the fuck are you shouting at you complete prick?'

But before Jack could finish his sentence, he could sense a crowd rushing towards him. He turned around and took a deep breath as he saw at least 20 or 30 men with cameras and microphones swarming his personal space.

'Jack, is it true that you ditched your fiancé just to have sex with prostitutes in Thailand?'

'Have you been tested for AIDS yet?'

'Are you going to marry that whore in the video?'

'What in the actual fuck are you fleabags yammering about?' Jack asked no one in particular. 'You don't know anything about me'.

'Who was better in bed? Your wife-to-be, or the Asian hooker?'

'Jack - can I get an exclusive interview?'

'No! Get away from me. Let me through'.

Jack pushed past the reporters as hard as he could but there was an audience of at least one hundred people behind them. Mainly women, it seemed, and they were jeering him and he could read one banner that said,

'You piece of shit, fuck off back to Thailand!'

His head was spinning and he had never felt this confused and angry all at once. Then an all too familiar voice rang out in his ears, 'Welcome back you cheating little cunt, where's your whore now?

It was Debs..

Jack was totally confused as to how this had happened but Debs pulled him to one side and started talking. 'So, I shared that clip of you and that ugly trollop in bed and it seems the whole of the world were as disgusted as I was!'

He swivelled round to see that the conversation was being filmed.

More insults started to come his way.

'Jack are you a paedophile?'

'Has your cock fallen off yet?'

He turned back to Debs and did his best to apologise. 'I'm sorry Debs, it's true that I never loved you, but that girl in the video is nothing to me'.

She looked confused but there was a glimmer of hope on her heavily made up face.

'What, you don't care for her then?'

Jack replied, 'That's right but I did meet another girl there, her name is Ice'.

With that news, Debs face turned into a fierce snarl and she pushed him hard enough to drop him to the ground.

'You go girl!'

Standing up and moving away from the furious woman, Jack blurted out,

'Fuck me, what is this? The Jerry Springer Show?'

There was whooping from the crowd and Jack decided that he had better get the fuck out of there before he completely lost his shit.

One hour later, he was in a taxi heading back to Wallingford. Even the bloody taxi driver recognised Jack. 'What just happened?' He thought, as the taxi driver, seemingly reading his thoughts, handed over his iPhone for Jack to see. On the driver's Facebook page, Jack recognised his own form in a blurry mini movie scene.

So, it transpired that the Facebook Live video had gone viral. Debs had shared it to her friends and they'd followed suit. By the time he had landed at Heathrow, it was national news. Shaun had really done a fucking number on him. The local rags had tipped off a few of the lowbrow tabloids and they absolutely adored this type of shit storm.

Jack's phone was ringing. This time he decided to pick up, hoping it was Ice.

'Son, please don't come home, we don't need this rubbish, not now'.

It was his Dad, always distant and now he sounded downright hostile. It made sense.

He couldn't go back to Debs house, obviously. Thankfully a friend had already offered him a place to crash for a few days.

As the taxi pulled up in a South Wallingford housing estate, Jack collected what was left of his thoughts and knocked on his buddy's front door.

Reality Bites

'What the fuck happens now?'

He said to nobody in particular and became reacquainted once more with the sofa that he'd spent many nights on previously.

Talk about some fucked up dreams.

First, he was back in bed with his lovely Ice and just as they were going to do the deed, the door was kicked in by an eight foot tall creature made up of Sparky's body and Debs' head. He scrambled to safety only to be stopped in the hotel corridor by over one thousand journalists, expect these were Thai versions of their British counterparts.

Running down the stairs he found his path blocked by a couple making mad passionate love. He instantly recognised the male half of this sordid act as none other than that shit bag Shaun and the female, well of course, she was the Thai strumpet that had started this utter shit storm in the first place.

Waking up in a pool of sweat, Jack sat bolt upright and as he opened his eyes, for real this time, Peter, his temporary surfing sofa host, was looking at him with a quizzical expression.

'Jack, you okay mate?'

Instead of replying, he grabbed Peter's laptop and started searching through the Thai news websites, hoping to hear some news, bad or good, regarding his missing friend. There was nothing, not even a footnote. To be fair, he would prefer no news than bad news, but Jack spent another 30 minutes trawling through the drab sites until Peter decided to speak up.

'Jack, I know you would prefer to keep your head down, but why not speak to one of those reporters?'

Before Jack could reply, he went on.

'At least use them to let the world know what happened to Chilli, maybe it will help to find the poor fucker?'

He had a point, Jack had to accept that much.

Two hours later there was a knock on the door and Johnny let in a weaselly looking young man who worked for the Daily Shitbag. Jack had agreed to one exclusive interview, but he needed this just as much as the tabloids did, for two reasons:

They had offered him two grand and fuck knows he needed some dosh right now

He could use the platform to raise awareness for Chilli

Okay, he could be a little shit at times and wouldn't give a stuff if one of the others had been dragged off, but that wasn't really the point. Chilli had been dealt a crap hand in life and had folded his last cards back there in South East Asia. At the very least, Jack vowed to do something to ensure he wasn't entirely forgotten.

'Okay Jack, where shall we start?'

He looked at the parasitic reporter who had a fake smile fixed on his pimply face and gave him the story that he so badly wanted.

* * *

She had only been away from her man for a few days but, for Ice, it felt like eternity.

Right now, she had to return to the job that had kept her in this God forsaken place. She had vowed not to bug him and so far, she'd managed to stay cool. But on the fourth day, after she had read news concerning him and his ex-fiancé, it was proving too much to bear. There was even an article in one of the Thai newspapers and lots of photos of the once happy couple. The sketchy video of Jack and that skanky Beach Road whore was something that she could do without seeing every time she went online.

The saving grace was that apart from Nok, none of her co-workers had realised that this cheating foreign bastard was in fact, the love of her life.

Despite the fact that girls in The Industry were hard as fuck, they still believed in the magic and stability of marriage. Surely this man was the absolute dregs and any whore that took him from his fiancée and family, well, they would have to answer to Buddha one day.

They hadn't really shaken hands on the agreement that would take her back home until he returned. Many times before, Ice had been promised a similar deal and each time, once the man went home, she never heard back.

'Ah fuck this shit' she said aloud and decided to break her 'Jack fast' and call the man, right now.

He picked up quicker than she could have hoped and for some dumb reason, nerves took over and she hit the red button and threw her battered phone across her room.

Long after the reporter had left Peter's house, Jack sat motionless and had never felt as confused.

It wasn't the fact that his sordid bullshit story would soon be spread all over every other breakfast table in the UK, and quite possibly beyond. Neither was it because, after a terse and short phone call, it seemed that his parents had, once more, disowned him. No, it was because a person 6000 miles away had thrown his emotions into turmoil.

To make matters worse, she hadn't even bothered speak to him this time. It was as if Ice had somehow developed a switch that could effortlessly fuck with his feelings whenever she felt like it. Jack had purposefully tried to shut this woman out of his mind since the plane had landed. That hadn't been so hard considering the utter chaos that had awaited him back in the airport. He'd not really had time to feel bad about the whole scenario, even when he had laid it on thick for the reporter, not one ounce of guilt had been experienced.

But when her fucking name had appeared on his phone, for just a moment, his life had been turned upside down, just like the first time they had met back in Pattaya.

'I have to see her again!'

Peter was upstairs but heard him quite clearly and came down in an instant. 'Mate, I know how you feel, well not exactly but…yeah'. His sentence drifted off and the man looked wistfully through the window and imagined coconut trees and warm smiling faces instead of the harsh factory laden skyline that was laughing back at him.

'I know that the poor fucker could be dead and I also know that nobody here gives a shit'.

Jack motioned him to continue.

'I reckon you should try and find out what happened to him'.

Jack had made a plea via his newspaper interview for Chilli but didn't really hold out much hope. He'd also left a message with both the Police force, useless cunts, and the British Embassy. Neither had replied and he didn't really expect much to happen.

Chilli wasn't rich and he certainly wasn't famous. He'd also been in prison before so the pigs were less than interested in helping this lost cause. But that wasn't the point. Chilli had fucked up royally but he certainly didn't deserve what came next.

Jack's phone was beeping again. His heart rate increased by 20% as he picked it up. Maybe she had decided to message him after all?

The text message was quite the opposite. He hurled the phone across Peter's lounge.

'What's up mate?'

'My toe rag of a boss just fired me…'

It was no surprise as the bloke was a distant relative of Shaun and Debs and obviously this was going to happen at some point.

'Never mind mate, fuck him and fuck them, let's get you a flight booked right now!' Nodding in agreement, it was the only place that Jack could think of.

Like many men before and, no doubt, after him, Jack had fallen for the Eastern charm that Thai woman seem to have in abundance. They know just how to 'take care' of their men whether they are customers or not and it's estimated that around 80 %, if not more, single men will return to Thailand after their first trip is over. If you take a look around the departure lounge at Suvarnabhumi airport, it is likely that there will be a lot of unhappy faces already planning their next trip. They are hooked and, most probably, their lives will never be the same again – for better or worse.

* * *

'Hello Love, do you like sucky fucky?'

It was hardly Bill Shakespeare but Ice had heard worse opening lines. The man asking her this question was a typical White Buffalo, but he was also holding several purple persuaders, AKA 500 baht notes, and this made him very attractive.

Ice had put the money from Jack aside for her family, and apart from a few hundred, she was on the bones of her beautiful arse once more, so she didn't need to be asked twice. All thoughts of Jack and some fucking futile future had left the building. He hadn't returned her call and neither did she expect him to. As she skipped off to some shitty hotel with this half man half Wildebeest, it was business as usual back in Sin City by the Sea.

* * *

The next day in Wallingford, Jack was looking online for cheap flights to Thailand. Things had gone from bad to worse since the newspaper article had seen the light of day. To be fair though, the tabloid had been true to their word and had even bumped his fee up to five whole grand. They'd sold a shitload of copies and he'd really laid it on thick.

The Police still hadn't returned the calls or email. Jack had even paid the local station a visit but it was only open three days a week.

Debs family had paid a few visits to Jack's parents and had implied that his head would be removed from his shoulders if he ever appeared in their neighbourhood again.

There had never been a better time to get on a plane and simply get the fuck out of dodge.

And that, was exactly what he did.

End of Chapter Three

▲ *Family at work – Photo by Paul Eddie Yates Photography*

Chapter Four
SWIFT RETURN

Jack had two things on his mind. Firstly, he would look for Chilli. Truth told, he didn't hold out much hope for the poor bastard, but at least he deserved an effort. Secondly, well, he needed to reconnect with Ice and take things to the next level.

The thought of going back to Wallingford, or anywhere in the UK, filled him with dread. His parents had long since lost interest in him and it seemed that his cards had been marked by Debs and her extended inbred family.

So maybe he was hanging absolutely everything on that bar girl who was possibly sucking off some German right at that moment.

* * *

Unlike most bar girls, Ice didn't trust banks or Western Union. So, when it was time for her to send money back to her village, she preferred to do it in person. She had saved up 10,000 baht to help her family pay for her sister's University fees. The money was there but, Jack notwithstanding, she had already forgotten the faces of the men that had been a part of the transactions.

Ice would get the overnight bus and that took an utter age to reach Buriram City. From there it was another two hour journey on local transport, usually an open backed taxi.

Her parents still hated the fact that their eldest daughter slept with men for money. Despite the fact that it was her cash that kept their youngest's dream of becoming a teacher alive. It was hardly unique, over half of the girls in the village, and a few boys, were working in the Industry either in Bangkok or Pattaya.

Swift return

Thankfully they would usually skirt around the topic until the visit was drawing to a close. Then, as regular as clockwork, her Dad would get shit faced on Yah Dong, a cheap but potent rice whisky infused with all kinds of herbs and whatnot, until he became so maudlin that he'd wail for hours. In contrast, her Mother would stay quiet and simply lay on the guilt with those withering stares until it was time for Ice to go back to Pattaya for another stint of mattress backed activities.

She packed her things and locked up her shithole of an apartment and walked towards the end of the Soi where she'd get a motorcycle taxi to Pattaya Bus Station.

* * *

Now back in Thailand, Jack had also learned that Shaun was also flying over in the near future. He'd bragged that he had met someone so special he was already thinking of bringing her back to meet his parents. The thought of bumping into him over here really interested Jack but he put that particular scenario on the back burner for now.

The taxi driver was the same one as the first trip. Although he was here less than a week ago, everything seemed different. Jack certainly wasn't a Pattaya veteran. For fucks sake, he'd only been here for a shade over four days, but things certainly looked clearer this time around.

He was no longer a first-timer, unsure of what to expect. The worst and the best had happened and he was back for a second helping. What else could possibly go wrong?

The plan was fairly simple, once he reached the hotel, he would start looking for Ice, and then she could help him look for Chilli. He also needed Frank's help.

The taxi driver had ignored his pleas to blast the air-conditioning and it was a sweaty mess, the plastic seat covers making things worse.

They reached Pattaya in super quick time and, although it looked very different and somewhat drab in the daytime, his heart fluttered a little as he started to recognise familiar landmarks.

Jack had not slept since the plane had taken off back in London and, right now, he was playing around with his phone and staring out of the window. Suddenly he saw a familiar face dart past on the back of a motorcycle taxi.

Some say that Thai ladies all look the same, but that simply was a crock of shit, Ice's finely chiselled and delicate features were one of many reasons he had fallen so hard in the first place.

It was her! Fucking had to be!

The motorbike was already almost out of sight.

'Stop the fucking car!'

Thanks to the shitty traffic, the taxi had all but slowed down to a snail's pace. Throwing the taxi driver his fare, clutching his rucksack Jack was ready to jump ship.

'Bok Sheepai!' (Thai slang for son of a bitch!'), the driver swore under his breath. But Jack had already flung the door open and was running after the small but fast motorbike like Usain Bolt.

'Ice!'

'Ice!'

There was no way on hell's earth that he was catching her on foot. As the bike started to disappear, he looked left and saw a bunch of motorcycle taxi drivers chilling out. Less than 30 seconds later, thanks to a purple persuader of his own, the chase was on. Jack hung on for dear life and his heart felt as if it would leap out of his mouth and onto the scorching tarmac. The bike kept up a breakneck pace and then, after three minutes, started to slow down.

Swift return

'No!'

'For fucks sake don't stop!'

But it was no use. Perhaps the motorbike lad was hungry or thirsty. Jack fished around for more Thai money but then realised that the place where they had stopped was a bus terminal. Removing his helmet, the young lad had a wide smile and pointed towards a queue that snaked halfway around the ramshackle building.

'Your lady, she there'.

He was pointing towards Ice.

She was still oblivious to the daredevil actions of her White Buffalo until he belted out a shout that would have woken the dead, back in Wallingford.

'ICE IT'S ME!'

She turned to face him and for a second, he could have sworn that she was crying. He ran over to the queue and held her in his arms. They kissed for twenty seconds and even the most hardened old crone sitting on a nearby bench looked impressed. She'd seen it all and then some, but right now, this was top drawer entertainment and it was free.

Well that had been some surprise! One minute she was dreading the journey and now here she was, sat next to her real life Prince Charming. Jack had literally swept this Isaan girl off her feet and she had never felt so fucking overjoyed. She had tried to explain that she was going back to her village but that didn't seem to worry him.

Shit, she had literally begged her last serious farang boyfriend to come upcountry with her and the spoilt little cunt hadn't even considered it. To add insult to injury, before she had even got to the bus, he was already sticking his cock into her ex- best friend.

Men were all the same. Except, it seemed, for this one. Was Jack really this decent? She had no idea that he was even coming back to Thailand

and wondered what his game plan actually was? Well, they certainly had more than enough to discuss and she had a few questions to ask him.

Jack was loving every minute of this odd bus journey and when even the twat of a bus driver scolded him and Ice for having a cuddle, it didn't really annoy him. As he looked at the flat countryside rolling past, he started to understand that there was far more to this country than a few gogo bars and a bunch of sexual tourists.

Ice had her head on his shoulder and was fast asleep, he wondered what she wanted out of this fledgling relationship. Was she after money? She'd be shit out of luck if that was the case. Maybe she was playing the long game? Also a waste of her time.

His parents still lived in a council house and went on holiday to Bournemouth every year. Hardly fucking Mombasa was it? No, there would be zero inheritance and they'd probably outlive him. He had absolutely nothing material to offer her, nor to any woman, only his heart and devotion. That was hardly enough for Debs, however he'd eventually discover that this lady already was head over heels in love with him, for richer, or, more likely, for poorer.

Hours later, Ice awoke and almost instantly started tapping away on her Smartphone. There was a cool translation App that worked fairly well. She was a whizz when it came to asking him questions and, depending on the answer, she would tilt her head and look thoughtfully out into the Isaan countryside, as if she'd just been gifted a pearl of infinite wisdom.

Jack did his best to be truthful, although not always an easy task. When she asked him what Debs originally did for a job, her eyes almost popped out of her head when he said she worked in a bar back in Wallingford. He corrected her when she started asking how much Debs would charge for sex?

Swift return

There were many differences that divided their worlds and it wasn't going to be easy if this seemingly random coming together had a chance of surviving.

Even though she was with Jack, this bloody bus journey was as uncomfortable as she could remember. Thankfully it wasn't too hot and half of the trip was overnight.

She laughed at the way her man did his best to eat the low quality Thai food that was on offer when they stopped just outside Bangkok. Even the lukewarm water on the tin table was infested with flies. She stopped him just before he swallowed a mouthful, and scurried off to the service station shop to get a few cool bottles of clean mineral water and some snacks to tide them over for the rest of the endless journey. When they re-joined the bus, most of the passengers were already dozing off and she was relieved when Jack did the same.

There were two more stops before the bus finally reached its destination. As she watched Jack stretch and yawn, she checked her phone and marvelled at the fact that this ramshackle bus always arrived at exactly 6:24am. They jumped onto a 'Samlor' taxi and after an even bumpier 90 minutes they pulled up outside her family home.

Jack gave her a hug and as she looked back at her home, she jumped slightly when she realised both of her parents were standing four feet away. Smiling, they definitely were not.

Despite the thousands of foreign 'boyfriends' that hook up with Thai ladies, whether they are bar girls or not, surprisingly few bother to make the trip to their other half's hometown. The idea of the massive culture shock is usually more than enough to put paid to that notion. But if you ever travel into Isaan, there are farangs living amongst the locals and some of them even thrive. The secret to living in the boonies begins with trying to understand both the language and the way of life.

Many will find work as English teachers and a significant number decide to retire here. Far cheaper than life in Bangkok or Pattaya, whilst it is true that it is no way near as exciting, there is a certain charm to places like Udon, Korat, Kohn Kaen, Buriram, Roi Et, Buriram and the hundreds of Ban (Villages) between them that make up the Isaan province.

Jack walked across to who the man who he assumed was Ice's father and extended his right hand.

The Thai man took a step back, muttered something that sounded like 'Farang' and spat a lovely green lug onto the floor before turning around and walking back to the wooden house.

'Charming'

Jack said to nobody in particular.

Shit, he had played this particular scene out in his mind more than once on that hellish bus journey but none of them had ended like this. He was stinking and Ice, although she still looked as fresh as a daisy, wasn't exactly standing up for him. In fact, she looked as if she was close to tears.

He tried to pull her towards him but she just turned away and walked slowly towards her mother. She fell to the ground, prostrate at her mother's feet and started making a submissive noise. So much for the romantic big entrance…

After half an hour, Ice's father returned and this time he was carrying two small stools and a large bottle of whisky.

Ice stood up slowly, and this time, her mother embraced her and they retreated to inside the house.

He motioned for Jack to sit down and he didn't need to be asked twice. He poured a decent measure of the spirit into a tin mug and lit up a fag, taking a slug himself before refreshing the vessel and passing it over to the Englishman.

Swift return

Jesus this was some rough shit, thought Jack, but it hit the spot.

This was repeated for the best part of an hour until Ice emerged from the house.

Fucking Hell!'

Jack exclaimed; she had undergone a transformation. Every inch of makeup had been removed and her figure hugging clothes had been replaced by what can only be described as loose-fitting sack cloth trousers and baggy plain top.

She knelt down in front of her father, making no eye contact with either man. Her father seemed oblivious to Ice even being there at his feet as he rolled up what must have been his twentieth cigarette. This bloke was proper hard core, just like out of the old Kung Fu movies Jack had loved watching as a child.

There was a small commotion from the house and then the mother returned, this time with a tiny dog and two young women. They looked proper shy as Jack gave them both a smile. The mother less so.

For Jack, this was something he'd never come even close to experiencing. They looked like a family from hundreds of years ago. Of course, that wasn't the case.

Bringing him back to present day, he noticed a nice shiny motorbike and a slightly less new pick-up truck parked to the side of the house. Ice was really supporting the whole family, not just the student sister. They were living quite a decent life on her salary. Looking all around and taking in the surroundings, right at that moment, Jack was as far away from the shitty estate in Wallingford that he was raised in, as he had ever been in his life.

Eventually Ice stood up, grabbed Jack by the sleeve and the whole family walked back inside without uttering a single word.

It was as good as Ice could have hoped for. Her father was a person of action, not words, and the fact that he hadn't kicked Jack out was a miracle. In fact, they both had that same annoying trait whereby they would simply sit there without saying a fucking word.

Men...

By now they had shared some drinks and with the rest of her family all at home at the same time, things were working out just fine. Her mum had whipped up a real Isaan feast and now was time for everyone to sit down and catch up on what families did best. Everyone, including Jack, sat around the plates of food cross legged. Her sisters giggled as he reacted to the red hot Papaya salad and marvelled at how his white cheeks turned a fierce red after swallowing a chili whole. For Jack, well, this was something he had never come close to experiencing back in dreary Wallingford. The spiciness of the food was a reflection of the spicy Thai culture embodied in this home. He never appreciated that laughter and love were missing from his own life, until he witnessed it first-hand here with Ice's family and he knew that he wanted to be part of it.

The food was on another level to the fare served up at the Wallingford Thai restaurant. After the meal, her father was trying his best to have a conversation with Jack and, eventually, it was clear that the two of them would have a day out tomorrow.

'Papa, he like you and he want to show you off to his friends'.

This was new territory to Jack who was quite humbled by this attention.

Ice explained that the order of the day would be a chicken fight in the morning and a fishing competition in the afternoon. She used the translating app to ensure that Jack understood what was in store for him.

'But, what about you?'

Swift return

'I will stay with Mama and my sisters and we will wait for the big fish you are catching for us'.

Jack laughed as he remembered the only time he went fishing before was when he almost won a goldfish at the Wallingford fun fair.

Opening his eyes to a fierce sun breaking through the wooden blinds, Jack had been in more comfortable beds before but, for some reason, he had slept like a baby. Ice's family had set him up in the front room and by the time he had woken up, it seemed that the rest of the household were already up and getting busy. Ice brought him a hot and sweet cup of coffee and almost instantly returned to the kitchen.

Once he'd shaken off the heavy sleep, Jack pulled on a T shirt and shorts that he'd managed to find in his rucksack and walked through the house on tiptoes. He wasn't used to staying with another family and right now, he had no idea of what to expect. Shit, he'd rushed into this whole fucking scenario and was feeling a little concerned. Coming from a pretty cold family, it was unusual to be welcomed into a house with such warmth.

He'd really enjoyed the previous evening and even though the ethnic food was much more flavourful than he was used to, he could sense the love that Ice clearly felt for her parents and siblings. Both of her sisters were beauties and they had clearly inherited their mother's looks. Her father was a quiet man but he was obviously proud of his family, and quite rightly so.

The four women looked up as Jack entered the kitchen and it looked as if they were preparing for a party. He was to learn, over the next few days, that Isaan people really love a good sing song as much as anyone he had ever met.

Ice skipped over and walked him to the very back of the house where there was a large plastic barrel of water and a makeshift curtain.

'You are fucking joking?'

She giggled back and handed him a small bowl.

Ten minutes later he had cleaned himself in the most primitive way he'd ever experienced. But he felt fresh and alive and was really looking forward to the next few days.

For Ice, this was by far the best home visit she could remember and it was amazing the way that her family, even her Dad, had taken to Jack. Unlike her previous Thai boyfriends, this man was no drama queen and went out of his way to fit in, despite the massive cultural differences that he must be experiencing.

Tonight, there was to be a big party and her mum and sisters were hard at work with the preparations. She wasn't entirely sure for the reason or the theme for the party but she was going to show off her man, that much was for sure. Now if only she could get the bugger to open up a little more, her life would be perfect.

Jack went outside to get some air and noticed that Ice's father was hard at work already. The pickup truck was gleaming and in the back was a large cage that contained a very fierce looking cockerel.

'Gai boxing!' - Gai is Thai for chicken. The older man repeated and walked over to the fighting cock and lifted up the cage. Jack wasn't overly keen on getting any closer but before he knew it, Ice's father had picked it up and was bringing it over.

'Fuck this!' Jack said but stood his ground.

He didn't want people to think that the English are pansies, so he feigned disinterest as the bird got closer.

'Papa!'

Ice's scream cut through any tension and the raptor was returned to its cage.

'He take you chicken fight and then fishing – you okay Jack?'

Swift return

She pointed again to the bird and told him its name was 'Khaosai' This was in homage to a very famous Thai boxer that Jack had never heard of. To be totally honest, he was loving this as he had never spent quality time with his own father so he was quite looking forward to the day ahead.

Thai men, at least the older generation, adore boxing and gambling more than anything on earth. So the combination of both is akin to religion all over the kingdom.

One hour later, after a huge breakfast, the two men set off and they were waved off by the remaining family. Jack laughed as he looked back at the four Thai ladies, it was if he and this chap were going into battle.

It was 11am by now, and the temperature was already almost 40 degrees Celsius. Wearing his favourite Manchester City shirt, Jack was sweating his nut sack off and wondered how people could live in this heat.

Ice's dad stopped the car at a fairly modern looking service station and looked straight at him.

'Pom choo Somchai!'

Jack had no fucking clue what that meant but smiled anyway. This was repeated four times until he finally got it.

His name was Somchai.

Jack was chuffed at the lack of formality and attempted a Thai bow, known as a 'wai'. This pleased Somchai greatly and he rolled up a few cigarettes for them to enjoy. He then climbed out of the truck and went into the garage shop for five minutes. Emerging with two bottles of the grog they had drank the previous evening and four bottles of soda water.

'Fuck me', thought Jack, 'Proper hardcore'.

He wasn't wrong.

30 minutes later they pulled over from the main road and followed a really bumpy dirt track for a few more miles.

Eventually they stopped just short of what looked like a small forest and after carefully lifting the cage out of the back of the truck, they walked into the trees. Jack was starting to think that he'd bitten off more than he could chew but after another five minutes, the trees thinned out and he started to hear voices. There were at least 50 people there, all middle aged and, by the sounds of it, they were already three sheets to the wind.

Placing the cage down gingerly, Somchai poured them both a stern fix of the whisky and topped it up with the now warm soda water. He found a huge ice bucket and dropped a handful of cubes into each tumbler.

By now the crowd started to gravitate towards the pair. It appeared that foreigners weren't very common in these parts. Far from being nervous, Jack was loving the attention and did his best to greet everyone. Placing both hands together, in the traditional Thai way, and placing them on his forehead, he bowed whilst saying,

'Sawasdee Krup'.

This amused the hell out of the assembled throng and they took it in turns having their photos taken with him. Glasses were topped up, and pretty soon, it was party time in the boonies. His Manchester City shirt was getting a lot of attention as many of the lads were letting him know in no uncertain terms who their favourite teams were. Everyone had an opinion, and they trash-talked the players just like they did back home.

But eventually, as always, the locals got bored of Jack and their focus turned back to the serious sport in hand. Jack was fairly tipsy and he was happy to take a seat as the spectacle started to begin. The seats were assembled in an oval shape and the first fight was announced. Jack was surprised to see that Somchai had already entered the gladiator's circle with Khaosai, minus his cage. Khaosai was a handsome beast and his feathers were as black as night apart from a white mark on his chest.

Jack managed to get a seat as the other combatant entered the ring of poultry pugilism. Both owners carried their fighting cocks to the

Swift return

centre of the ring and then all hell broke loose. Jack noticed that money was changing hands and the adrenalin that he used to feel at City games started to take over his whole body.

They were at it like a pair of mini feathered Mike Tysons and Jack joined in with the excited crowd as each man yelled his head off in support of their favourite.

Then, just as suddenly as it began, the battle ended. Jack was dismayed to see that Khaosai was no more. He was transformed from a proud and fierce fighter into a limp and pathetic twitching mess. The other bird had managed to break its neck and the combat was over for these two. Jack drained his glass as he trudged after Somchai.

As they carried the carcass back to the truck, he noticed that the older man wasn't in the slightest bit bothered. He would learn later that Somchai had bet heavily on the other bird. Tossing the body into the back of the truck, Somchai looked at Jack and chuckled as he said, 'Khaosai Die Lao' – literally meaning – the cock's fucking dead mate...

It was a bloody shame, but Jack was hardly David Attenborough, and just felt good to be part of the boys days out. This was a lot of fun and Jack would have happily stayed but Somchai had other plans. Another couple of chaps walked over and as they climbed into their truck, he motioned for Jack to follow suit and pointed to the fishing gear.

Jack was wondering if the older man should be driving but he didn't have to worry too long as police sirens started to sound and four cars with lights flashing appeared as if out of nowhere.

'Tumluat!'

Jack guessed that this was Thai for Old Bill and the scenes back at the cock ring confirmed that the shit had just got real. People were running in all directions as if their lives were at stake, and only the cock owners remained as they were torn between fleeing the scene or losing their prize fighting wards.

The Policeman nearest to them started talking to Somchai, it was clear that he was on first name terms and things weren't too heated until he produced a very old device that looked like a breathalyser from the 1980s. Somchai was starting to get flustered and Jack felt bad for the man. He approached the policeman and gave him his best 'Sawasdee' complete with a very exaggerated wai.

This had little effect, but the policeman's colleague chuckled and then pointed at the City shirt that Jack had on. Turned out he was a massive fan of the team and the conversation soon changed to a far more important topic. Somchai started to relax and was also now pointing at the shirt. Jack laughed.

'You want this shirt?'

The policeman certainly did. It was a bargaining point and when Jack removed the sweaty garment and passed it over to the Thai City fan, things got a whole lot more chilled. Ten minutes later, the pair of them were driving away with the other fisherman in tow.

Jack half expected to see a tiny lake or maybe a canal for the fishing expedition so he was a little more concerned when faced with a very wide and fast flowing river. Instead of sitting on the bank, the four men were to use a large raft that was anchored by a small pier. This was the Mun river and had very little resemblance to the Thames that flowed through Wallingford.

Less than 20 minutes later, they had paddled to a point that was deemed to be halfway across and the large weight was dropped to ensure that they stayed put. Drinks were poured and, to Jack's surprise, a small barbeque device was lit. Amongst the food that was presumably going onto the barbeque, Jack was shocked to see the prone body of Khaosai.

The other two fellows were called 'Paiboon' and "Samran". Somchai made the introductions and the days fishing finally kicked off. Samran was the designated chef and got to work as he plucked the once gladiator cock with a huge smile on his face.

Taking a sip of the liquor, Jack realised that this wasn't Thai whisky, or at least not the version he had been drinking earlier. Somchai picked up on this as Jack almost heaved on the first shot.

'Yah- Dong'

He repeated this until it was old news.

For Jack, the drink had a strong herby flavour with an afterburn that just wouldn't quit. He drained the rest of the glass over the side and started to watch the two men who were already getting stuck into the fishing, or at least that's what they called it.

'Tok Pla,' said the older one as he hoisted a hook laden with bloody meat over the side of the raft. No rods were used, just a very thick handline and this started to disappear as the current took it away.

This didn't look too difficult, thought Jack, and he accepted as Somchai baited his hook for him.

By the size of the fucking hook, they weren't trying to catch minnows, in fact it looked more like they were after something much bigger.

All four men had their lines in the water and, just in case they got a bite, they were tied around a stout box near the centre of the craft. Paiboon was sat on the box and he'd almost plucked poor old Khaosai bald by now.

The Barbeque was fired up and all four men were puffing away on some very strong Thai tobacco, drinking in the beautiful scene across the river and beyond. Jack did his best to converse with the trio, and although it was a waste of time and oxygen, at least he was making the effort.

Fuck, thought Jack, Chilli would have capsized the fucking raft and swam back to shore by now. He started to wonder where his missing buddy may be and made a promise to nobody in particular to call Frank later that day to see if he'd resurfaced, dead or alive.

His train of thought was rudely interrupted as the entire raft started to move with a sudden jolt. Judging by the actions of Somchai, he'd hooked a massive fish. With Paiboon and Samran holding him by the waste, Ice's father gripped the thick line with both hands and pulled with all his might. Jack tried to help but here wasn't enough line for him to grab onto so he just assumed a cheerleading role instead.

Somchai was playing it cool as he was still puffing on the roll up as if he was simply hanging out the washing. That was his undoing as he let go with one hand and grabbed the half glass of Yah dong and took a swig. For half a second, he was the coolest man on the boat, and then, with a massive tug, whatever was on the other end of the line pulled him off the boat and into the fast moving river.

Jack was stunned for a moment and when he realised that Paiboon and Samran weren't going to dive in, he lowered himself into the water and, using the line as a safety device, started making his way towards Somchai. By now, the poor man had let go of the line and was being swept away by the strong currents of the Rover Mun.

'He can't fucking swim!' Said Jack aloud.

Indeed, Ice's dad was doing a great impression of a drowning rat, and Jack, still holding the line, started to kick his legs in an effort to catch him before he disappeared under the current. Thanks to some rudimentary lifeguard lessons, Jack reached his man and brought the knackered Somchai back to the raft where the two useless tossers made an attempt to help them back aboard. They achieved this without spilling a drop of Yah Dong, much to their credit. They then returned to the task of catching the evil Leviathan who was halfway to Laos by now.

* * *

Swift return

Ice was helping her mum in the small garden at the side of the family home when the men returned.

'Jack, what happened?'

As they climbed out, the whole female contingent of the family were stood in awe as they had never seen their father and husband in such a joyous mood.

Ice's mother was preparing herself to chide her husband as she could smell the unmistakable stench of Yah Dong drifting her way. But before she could get a single word out, he started talking, ten to the dozen, what a brilliant day it had been.

Ice felt intense pride as it appeared that Jack had not only saved her dad from a watery grave, but he'd also bribed the local police into letting Somchai off from a large fine and possible imprisonment for Cock fighting and drunk driving.

Her mum wasn't quite as impressed and made a few noises because there didn't seem to be any fish for their dinner. At this, Somchai turned around and started pulling the largest catfish any of them had ever seen from the back of the pickup. The bloody thing was over two metres in length and even his betrothed was silenced into admiration, something that hadn't happened since their wedding night all those years earlier.

The men took the fish around the back to the same shower where Jack had bathed just this morning. They laid it across several barrels and started scraping off the skin and preparing fillets for supper.

Somchai handed Jack a long thin knife and pointed to the belly of the beast. Jack understood that he was being given the honour of slicing through the gut and took a deep breath as he tried to cut a straight line in a single pass. Once the fish had been cut open, the men reached inside and pulled out the bloody intestines and let them drop into a bucket on the ground.

Somchai, having caught catfish in the Mun for decades, started to sift through the guts, looking to see if the fish had consumed anything valuable that it couldn't digest. Catfish are known to clean the rivers by eating whatever garbage they can find. It wasn't unusual to find bottle tops, or even keys that unlucky fisherman dropped into the water. Today Somchai was stunned by what he found, and attributed the treasure to the good juju brought by the new member of his family, who, though he had only been with them one day, was proving to be a worthy addition.

Looking around to make sure that the ladies weren't watching, Somchai washed off his bloody hands and held up a delicate silver ring for Jack to see. Placing it into Jack's pocket, Somchai then embraced Jack with tears in his eyes and said, many times,

'Pom Lookchai Jack, Pom Lookchai Jack!' ''Jack, my son!'

This was almost too much for Ice to take as she realised, Jack was certainly the fucking real deal.

'Jack, my father, he always wanted a son'.

This was both a shock and a real pleasure for him to hear.

Needless to say, the fish fed the whole family and plenty of guests to boot. Jack had never enjoyed a day and evening so much and he was dead certain that this was the way he wanted to bring up his own family, with Ice. It was at that moment that he realised that he was in love with her and was already thinking of ways to delay his return to monotonous reality back home. He knew without a shred of doubt that he wanted her to wear the catfish ring on her finger for all of eternity.

The next day, Ice listened as well as she could, with her translation app working overtime, whilst Jack told her his thoughts. She was overjoyed because she'd felt this way for some time. Now that Jack had been accepted into her family, she thought for possible ways to keep him here. Then she remembered her mum talking about the shrimp farm that a family member, Ice's uncle, was thinking of selling. The farm was doing well but uncle also had two fish farms and didn't have time to run all three concerns.

Jack seemed keen and the pair of them took the family motorbike to check it out. Uncle Pichit was a small wiry man who was a lot darker than the rest of Ice's extended family but he looked friendly and he happily showed them around the shrimp farm. In all fairness it wasn't much more than a few large paddling pools filled with water and different sized shrimps in each one. But it turned a decent profit.

He only wanted around 300K baht for the lot and that included the small plot of land. Jack was feeling bullish and tried to knock him down and managed to get an offer of 250K accepted. That was near enough £6500, not a figure to be sniffed at but seemed doable by Christmas. They shook on the deal and stayed for lunch and a few beers.

'Ice, I am really happy here, how are you feeling?'

Ice smiled back and leant over to kiss him on the lips.

As they rode home, Jack could feel his phone vibrating. He waited until they arrived and read the message out loud.

'Jack, this is Frank, when are you coming down? Shaun is here and I have set him up a beauty for the shit he pulled on you and Chilli'.

Jack was brought back down to earth and had some thinking to do.

That night they made passionate love, for the first time without any protection, and even though they kept it quiet, the couple orgasmed together noisily and held each other until they were both sound asleep.

Over breakfast, Ice's sisters, Nam and Oot giggled as the lovebirds sat down and marvelled at how their older sister was positively glowing like never before.

'Ice, I have to go to Pattaya for a few days before I fly back home, can we talk please?'

She didn't want Jack to leave her but listened as patiently as she could while Jack did his best to reassure her it was for the best. He explained that Frank was helping him look for Chilli and that he didn't want Ice to be at risk.

'I know that fucker Sparky has the hots for you and I really can't let anything bad happen, not now darling'.

'But Jack, I want to look after you'.

Eventually, she accepted and they rode into Buriram to exchange some money that Jack wanted to leave her with, plus a small deposit for Pichit. He promised her that he wouldn't be led astray whilst back in Sin City and she reluctantly believed him.

Thrusting a piece of paper in his hand she said, 'This my friend Nok, she can help you'.

They cuddled for an hour and it went so fast, when Somchai fired up the pickup truck, both of them were almost in tears.

'I will FaceTime you when I get there darling'.

Steeling herself for his departure, Ice knew that there was a lot of waiting ahead of her but at least, this time, she wasn't going back to Pattaya.

End of Chapter Four

▲ *At the Flower Market - Photo by Paul Eddie Yates Photography*

Chapter Five

REVENGE IS A DISH BEST SERVED BY A LADYBOY

After the short flight to Bangkok from Buriram, Jack took a bus to Pattaya and had some time to reflect on his life. Boy had it changed! He felt bloody sad and happy at the same time, he'd never experienced these emotions with Debs. This time it was for real. Okay, Christmas was over half a year away but he had a plan, and this one was worth sticking to. It went a little like this:

1. Find work.
2. Save every penny except the £250 he would send back to Ice every four weeks.
3. Do research into shrimp farming and also something called permaculture that he'd read some months earlier.
4. Speak to his parents about that 'nest egg' they once mentioned.
5. Return to Thailand on Christmas eve and finally start to live his life.
6. Marry Ice in an elaborate ceremony which would rival Harry and Megan's recent extravaganza.

* * *

Meanwhile back in deepest Pattaya, Shaun was having a high old time with Mimi and was thinking of marriage plans himself. He even suggested to his love that they go and visit his/her parents upcountry, secretly intending to pop the question during the visit.

'Oooh honey, cannot!'

Mimi continued, 'Mama and Papa don't like me work here in Pattaya; they say it very bad place'.

This pissed off Shaun no end and he went off in a strop for the rest of the evening. In fact, he wanted to make a point so instead of going back to the hotel, where he had invited Mimi to stay, he went out drinking alone.

Revenge is a dish best served by a Ladyboy

Finding himself on Soi 6, he remembered that Envy was a favourite hangout for the old bloke they had met on the plane, what was his name again? Shaun was three sheets to the wind when he saw the man himself with a bevy of beauties sat around him. It was as if they were hanging on his every word. One of the things he loved was that in Pattaya, the bar girls were just so fucking down to earth and friendly.

Soi 6, also known as Soi NightWish, had many such businesses lined up on either side. He ordered a beer and watched Frank for a few minutes before approaching him. Thinking that this guy may have a problem with the way Shaun handled himself last time with Chilli and Jack, he was a little cautious. He needn't have been.

Frank looked up and spotted Shaun, hard to miss with his cruel beak of a nose and the near two metre frame that was wobbling towards him with an awkward grin. He would usually give anyone the benefit of the doubt, but this prick, well he had fucked over two of his so-called friends already and that really did not sit well with the older man.

But Frank was a sly one, when it was needed. Instead of telling this scum bag to fuck off, he decided to play the long game. There was a chance that he knew were Chilli was and also, he deserved some real payback for the Facebook/YouTube video that had made a laughing stock of Jack.

'Shaun isn't it?'

He ushered him over and moved along the sofa so Shaun could sit down.

'Frank mate, great to see you! And who are these lovely ladies?'

That sealed it for Frank, how could someone be so two-faced? They shared a few beers as Frank thought hard for appropriate payback for Chilli and Jack. He texted Jack whilst in the toilets and was chuffed to hear that he would be in Pattaya the next day.

'Come on son, lets hit a few more bars'

Shaun had all but forgotten about Mimi and was even paying Frank's drink tab.

They ventured down Soi 6, stopping in Kawaii bar and a few other quality establishments before walking down the second road and into Soi LK Metro.

'I like to have a few in Touch a gogo. My mate Dave Samuel runs the place and he's a top lad for an Ozzie, and an Arsenal fan to boot'.

Shaun would have gone anywhere, he was getting shit faced, that was when he started opening up to Frank. Over a few black sodas in Touch, Frank learnt that Mimi had stolen Shaun's heart and wasn't really interested until he saw a few photos of the ladyboy.

'Mimi is the only woman I've met so far who really turns me on. She is not delicate as the other bar girls I've been seeing here in Pattaya. Her tits are incredible and somehow she knows exactly what I like - she finds my most sensitive spots,' Shaun bemoaned.

'She's very beautiful', Frank said without a hint of irony in his voice.

'I know, but we had an argument and I'm scared she will leave me'.

After listening for ten minutes, Frank put his hand on Shaun's shoulder and, with a huge grin, said,

'Well Shaun, I think I know how you can show your love for him, I mean Mimi'.

Shaun thought he misheard at first so he was all ears,

'Get a tattoo declaring your love for Mimi'.

Shaun was interested but a little cautious.

'I hate tattoos, always have'.

Frank was ready for this.

'Well, this will show that your love has no bounds'.

Shaun was thinking about this when Frank paid the bill and grabbed him to leave.

'Let's go over Walking Street way to Soi Diamond and kill two birds with one stone. Heaven above gogo is a banging place for some eye candy and there are plenty of tattoo parlours in the area.'

Shaun wasn't arguing, in fact he was fucking loving Pattaya. There wasn't a frown to be seen from these ladies and he'd almost forgotten that Mimi existed. Okay, it wasn't cheap but where was nowadays? They had a few rounds in Heaven above gogo and even Shaun was happy to pay for a few lady drinks, the dancers were so cute.

Typically, half of the money for the Lady drink will go into the girl's pocket and some of the time, the drinks are a small shot of generic spirit topped up with cola/soda. If you venture into a quality gogo bar such as Touch/Heaven Above, you will have a great time, but in order to ensure that the best girls come and join you, order them a Lady Drink and you will be well away.

'Right young man, let's get you some ink!'

Shaun hadn't even noticed that Frank had already paid the bar bill and he was starting to feel more than a little pissed. They left the bar and walked back up to the bottom of Soi Diamond before taking a left.

'Frank, where did you get those tattoos mate?'

The older man had two full sleeves of designs that he only showed off when in Pattaya. Back home, well he wore long sleeved shirts because of the colder climate, plus he preferred to keep them covered when around the nosey bastards back home.

'Celebrity Ink is the place, but it's closed at the moment'.

It was approaching midnight but there were three small tattoo parlours next to each other just across the second road. Two were closed but the one in the middle was alive and kicking. They navigated across the busy junction and Frank asked Shaun to wait outside just to check that the place was actually open for business.

Whilst Shaun was kicking his heels outside, his phone started vibrating and he smiled as the message from Mimi appeared on the screen.

'Teelak, where you go, I miss you.'

So his love life was back on track and Frank was beckoning him to come inside. He was a little surprised to see that Frank was speaking Thai to the artist but he'd made up his mind, he was having this fucking thing done no matter what! Instead of answering Mimi, he pretended to ignore the message and plonked himself down in the tatty leather dentist style chair.

'So where do you want it Shaun?' Frank was even more excited than he was.

Holding out his left arm, Shaun grinned and pointed to the area just above his wrist.

'Okay, what do you want the tattoo to say?'

'I love Mimi'.

Fair enough, thought Frank and he spoke in rapid Thai to the artist who was already unwrapping a new needle in anticipation.

'Can we hurry this up please because I have pussy to attend to?'

'Fuck me,' thought Frank, he's keen this one.

The artist started up the kit and, without using a stencil, started writing away on Shaun's skin. Although he was playing the hard man, he couldn't quite bear to look at the tattoo process.

'Fucking smarts a bit', he grimaced through clenched teeth.

To be fair it was all over in 45 minutes and both the artist and Frank took a photo. When Shaun finally picked up the courage to look, he was dismayed.

'I can't understand that, it was supposed to be in fucking English not that foreign gibberish.'

Frank chuckled and replied .

'Well, it looks beautiful and your Mimi will appreciate it.'

Shaun seemed appeased, and after paying the artist, he said goodnight to Frank and made his way back to the hotel and Mimi. Frank was off to one of the many late night clubs in Pattaya but not before he pinged a message to Jack.

Shaun, for the life of him, couldn't find his fucking hotel. He stumbled as he tried to navigate his way into a side road and was pleasantly surprised to see a flashing red light just across the Soi. The light was bright enough to cut through his drunken haze and he wandered in and ordered a drink. It was a gogo bar and it was only after he had settled in that he realised there wasn't a single pair of tits on display. He nearly choked on his beer when he realised that the stage was full of handsome young men dancing around their individual poles.

'Hello Mistah, how are you?'

Shaun really wanted to get up and leave, but something inside him wouldn't let him go. The man had hold of his arm and was admiring his new tattoo. He fixed Shaun with a flirty gaze as he ran his finger down the still painful design.

'Is it true?' He asked.

Shaun plucked up the courage and replied, 'Yes I love very much'.

The man giggled in an effeminate way and continued,

'That's fine honey, I love it too'.

Shaun was a little confused and then asked the gogo boy,

'What is it that you love? 'Do you know Mimi too?'

The dancer mocked surprise and retorted,

'No honey, that isn't what your tattoo says'.

By now Shaun was getting peeved.

'Tell me, what the fuck does it say then?'

Releasing his arm and then placing Shaun's hand on his silky speedos, squeezing his ample groin, he replied,

'Cock!, it says I love Cock!'

Instead of pulling away, Shaun finally admitted defeat and pulled the man's head towards him for a kiss that he had been denying himself for more than 20 years as a closet homosexual. He had suppressed the urges and fears for his life entire. Now, confronted with the reality, he accepted his fate and felt his body respond to the male pole dancer who was pressing against his own pole. Here in Thailand, where nobody knew him, secrets were unravelling, and Shaun just couldn't be arsed enough to care.

Are ladyboy lovers gay?

Well, amongst Pattaya's 1,000 plus bars, it is rumoured that there are around 50 - 100 gay and ladyboy establishments. Many of them are located around the Boys Town areas but there are others dotted around Walking Street and between the Beach and Second Road. Married men have been known to come to Pattaya specifically to sleep with and hangout with Ladyboys.

Some Ladyboys are pre-op and some have had their genitalia removed. One thing is for sure, Ladyboys are usually a lot of fun and are utter drama queens. Anything seems to go in Pattaya and as they love to say in Thailand, whether you pick a girl, boy or ladyboy, it is totally 'up to you!'

End of Chapter Five

▲ *Hey, Sexy Man! - Photo by Paul Eddie Yates Photography*

Chapter Six
HOW THE MIGHTY HAVE FALLEN

Staggering up the stairs to his room, Shaun had forgotten why he was so pissed off in the first place. He opened the door gingerly to be met with a hard stare followed by a stream of Thai insults. 'Yed Mai Yed Por!' - Meaning Fuck your parents!

Shoes were thrown, threats were made, and Shaun feared for his own safety so he beat a hasty retreat and went downstairs for some breakfast. He had enough sense to cover up the 'I love cock!' tattoo with a long-sleeved shirt, but was struggling to walk without a limp as his arse was still hurting from the poundings that Thai Gogo boy had dished out earlier. He couldn't even remember if the man whore was wearing a condom, didn't seem to care at the time.

He was dumbstruck as to why Mimi was so pissed off, after all, he was the one in charge and if he wanted to go out for a few, what the fuck was the problem? Deciding to start early, Shaun ordered a beer and sat out on the restaurant balcony for some hair of the dog.

'Shaun you twat, what the fuck are you doing here?'

He turned around to see the familiar faces of Stuart and Gary, part of the Wallingford Posse that had started coming here decades ago.

'Fuck me, imagine seeing you two here!'

He instantly cheered up and moved over and sat down to join them.

'You ain't staying here are you?'

The way Gary asked him, instantly made Shaun feel uneasy.

'What if I am?' He demanded.

'Some nice sorts here'.

How the mighty have fallen

The pair exchanged glances and burst out laughing. They were going to let Shaun in on the secret when their attention was diverted to the elegant vision that appeared at the bottom of the hotel restaurant stairway. Instantly both of Shaun's friends swung around as they heard the stilettos on the fake marble floor.

'Look, there's one now!'

'Jesus H Christ, what a looker'.

Shaun looked up to see Mimi dressed to the nines. He was preparing to let his friends know that this was his girl when he noticed the pair of them were laughing.

'One of the best ladyboys I ever seen.'

'Almost nice enough to turn me queer!'

Shaun felt a hot flush run through him and got up to leave. What the fuck were they saying? Then it hit home. Every time he and Mimi had sex, it was either a blowjob or he had to take her from behind. One time he could have sworn that he felt stubble on Mimi's face and he had never heard a girl fart so loud and so often. The lights were always off and those tits were so firm, well he had never felt anything like it.

Mimi was a fucking Katoey! (Ladyboy)

The exit door was so close to where Mimi was standing but Shaun tried his best to get the fuck out of there before he was spotted. He nearly made it but literally two steps from freedom, in the highest pitch voice possible, Mimi screamed out

'Shaun honey, where you go? Let's go make love right now you naughty boy!'

He continued on his escape route but he could already hear the jeers from those two Wallingford dickheads ringing in his ears.

'Shaun, you faggot, just wait until we tell the others!'

'Yeah you little shit stabber!'

Shaun put his head down and kept on walking. Hours later, once the coast was clear, he returned to his room and thankfully all of Mimi's stuff was gone. His arse was hurting something chronic by now and when he checked his pants, he could see both blood and sperm stains.

'For fucks sake, why did I have to be queer?'

He shouted out and turned on the shower in an attempt to wash the gayness out of his system.

That bastard Frank must have known, hence the tattoo. His flight back home was still two days away. Opening the minibar, Shaun grabbed a bottle of Johnny Walker Black Label and did his best to drink away the last 24 hours.

***

'Hi Ice, yes I've just arrived here in Pattaya and I miss you too darling'.

It wasn't natural for Jack to tell somebody that he missed them but right now it felt totally normal. He planned to propose to her and place the catfish ring on her finger when he returned at Christmas time. His heart even felt a bit heavy when he said goodbye, but now he was meeting Frank with a view to finding out what happened to Chilli.

He'd booked two nights at The Eastiny Inn again and was waiting for the man to arrive. They'd arranged to meet at the Soi 8 bars opposite the hotel, and despite the amount of attention he was getting from those cute bar girls, he didn't feel tempted once. In fact, he showed off a photo of he and Ice taken days earlier, and even this didn't stop them trying to get into his pants.

'Jack, how the fuck are you?'

Frank was on the scene, and by the shouts of, 'Oh Papa, where you go?', he was something of a celebrity in these parts.

How the mighty have fallen

They shook hands as Frank ordered a round of drinks, plus three for the fittest girls in the bar.

'Just wait until I tell you what I did to Shaun'.

'To be honest mate, I couldn't give a fuck about that wanker.'

It was true, Shaun was long gone for Jack, and he was here for Chilli - and nobody else. But he could also see that Frank was a good man and seemed a little down when his story was cut short.

'Sorry Frank, tell me what happened, please'.

The older man perked up and spent a good ten minutes telling Jack the tattoo story.

'You are fucking joking right?'

'No mate, it's all true and I heard it through the grapevine that he was seen leaving on a motorbike in the wee hours from a gay gogo bar just off Soi 13/2'.

This was pure gold, Jack always wondered why Shaun had such a problem with gay people, now he knew why. Shaun was in total denial. But what a fucking way to come out of the closet.

'Jack, is that you mate?'

He looked around to see both Gary and Stuart from Wallingford were behind him.

Then for another fifteen minutes, he listened as they told him and Frank the absolutely hilarious scene they witnessed in the Penthouse Hotel.

'He's fucking done for, just wait until we tell the boys back home!'

Long after they had left, Jack was feeling a little torn because of what he'd just heard. Shaun was nothing to him but they had history and try as he might, Jack wasn't a total cunt. Frank sensed this and suggested they hit Soi 6, then LK and finally Heaven Above for some ping pong shows.

'Have you heard anything about Chilli?'

Frank replied, 'I've already put the word out for him. I think tonight, you need to relax a bit because tomorrow is going to be a long old day'.

'I don't suppose we can just call it a night?' Jack pleaded.

But Frank had already paid the bill and was hailing a Baht Bus down for the pair of them. If Jack hadn't seen the best of Pattaya's legendary nightlife before, he certainly had by the next day. As frequent visitor to the clubs, Frank was well known and loved, from the bars in Naklua, all the way to Jomtien and most of them in between. If Jack hadn't been in love, he would have let the girls take charge and do their best. Instead, he drank, and observed Frank working the bar with his silver tongue.

Jack was impressed by his command of Thai and also by the fact that Frank was already asking questions regarding Chilli. He heard the name 'Sparky' and 'Jet-ski' more than once.

By the time they had reached the strip in Jomtien, both men were plastered. They crashed down on some bamboo chairs outside the bar, it was still nice and warm and the sound of the waves crashing on the beach added to the chilled mood.

The serving girl was as cute as a button but when she brought their drinks, she did a wicked double take when she looked at Jack's face. She scurried off and Frank look at his younger companion with a wink and said, 'You're on a promise there mate!'

Jack hadn't even noticed; he was deep in text conversation with a beautiful young lady in Buriram.

'Fucking hell, you are properly smitten with that Ice bird, fair play to you.'

They drained the beers and Jack was going to suggest they call it a night, when the girl came back. This time she sat down and fixed Jack with a steely gaze.

How the mighty have fallen

'Jack, you forget me nah?'

'Ah Nok, how are you my friend?'

Instead of replying she asked him, 'Where is Ice?'

'Well she wanted me to contact you, she is staying in village now until I come back.'

Nok smiled and replied,

'That's good, here is not good place for her, not anymore.'

Jack was confused, he thought they were buddies. Then as he was ready to ask another question, he noticed the blood had run out of her lovely bronze face.

A deep voice broke out behind him.

'Hey Farang,, how are you?' It was Sparky!

Not waiting for an invite, the Thai man sat down and rolled up a cigarette whilst smirking at the surprise on Jack's face.

'Nok is mine now, and soon, I will take your girl, I will use her and throw her in the garbage.'

He went on.

'You farangs think you can come here fuck our women and then, when it goes wrong, you cry like little fucking babies'.

Both Jack and Frank stayed silent.

'You see, this is my bar and I have many businesses in Pattaya, I am a rich man. 'If I want something, I just take it.'

Jack really wanted to say something but he knew that this man was a troublesome fucker who just wanted an excuse to cause some serious shit.

With a cruel smile he wrapped up the one way conversation by saying,

'If you think I am joking, why not ask your friend Chilli, if you ever find his body!'

He cackled like an old witch, grabbed Nok by the arm and dragged her away.

The pair of Englishmen stayed silent until he left. Sparky had a huge Harley Davidson and only when the burbling of the twin exhausts had disappeared into the night down Jomtien Beach Road, did they continue their conversation.

'I fucking hate that bloke'.

Jack had real vitriol in his voice. He went on

'I know that Chilli was a plank but something needs to be done'.

Frank nodded as Jack continued his rant.

Instead of joining in, Frank threw in a curve ball.

'Jack, where are you lads from?'

It was true, neither man had really discussed their personal lives so far.

'Wallingford, ever heard of it?'

Frank laughed and replied, 'Heard of it? Jack, I lived there once'.

'You are shitting me?'

Frank leant forward and started telling Jack his connection with the small town in South Oxfordshire.

'So, going back to 35 years ago, I fell in love with a Thai lady who was living there'. Not exactly love at first sight and I had never been outside of the UK at that point'.

Jack leaned forward as he liked a good story as much as the next man.

'So to cut a very long story into a medium length one, we shacked up together and she became pregnant. But a month after giving birth to our son, she was murdered.'

'Fuck me!'

Jack never saw that one coming.

'She worked in the mental health hospital and one of the inmates did her in with a carving knife. Totally fucked my mind up, losing her.'

Jack was knocked back by this twist.

'And where is your son now?'

With a very sad face, Frank replied, 'No fucking idea. I went off the rails and by the time I realised, the fucking council took him away from me. By the time I got my shit together, he was long gone'

'But, you have never tried to find him?'

Frank lay back in his chair and replied, 'To be honest, I saw little point, they told me he was with a foster family and by then, I was already over here in Thailand.'

He concluded the story by telling Jack that he then moved here for a year, had a decent pay out for his wife's death, partially insurance and mainly from the hospital. He later moved back to the UK, drifted into a loveless marriage, and eventually back into the single life that was obviously agreeing with him.

'Frank, what did you do for a job back then?'

'Well, you won't believe me but I was a copper.'

Jack wasn't actually that shocked, Frank had a confident manner and knew how to handle himself.

'In fact, I did some voluntary work here and still have a few buddies in the Thai Police force.'

Hmmm thought Jack, that could be quite useful right now. As if he was a mind reader, Frank gave him a reassuring squeeze on his shoulder and finished up by saying,

'Way ahead of you, I have already tapped up a few of Pattaya's boys in brown regarding our mutual friends, Chilli and Sparky.'

That concluded the night's drinking and Frank hailed a meter taxi to take them to their respective hotels for the night. The next day, both were up and raring to go nice and early and met up for breakfast at Kiss Food and Drink on the Second Road.

European and American tourists are spoilt for choice when it comes to deciding where and what to eat in Pattaya. There are literally hundreds of bars and restaurants that offer a very good version of their favourite fayre whilst on holiday. The author's personal favourite for a killer breakfast is Rosie O'Grady's on Soi 7.

Before Jack could start discussing the best way forward, Frank beat him to the punch. 'Listen, I've spoken to my contacts and they are aware that Chilli is missing and also that Sparky is in the frame.' He went on, 'It's my gut feeling that Chilli is still alive because they haven't found any bodies since last month, or at least none that aren't already identified. Jack, did you say that Chilli was already reported as a missing person back home?'

'Yes but nobody really cares, he doesn't have any family and he has a criminal record. He's a loner'.

Frank looked a little perplexed and continued,

'Here's the rub, you will not like this.'

Jack got ready for the bad news.

'They have asked, no, they have instructed me to advise you not to look for him.'

'What the fuck?'

Jack was going to kick off but Frank interjected.

'I know Jack but it's good advice. You see, here in Thailand, we stand out. Even in Pattaya, where there are thousands of foreigners and wherever we go, there will be some Thai that has seen us. If we go in now with our size nines, well, Chilli will most probably end up in Jomtien bay as fish food, and the authorities have no way to guarantee your safety either.'

How the mighty have fallen

Jack listened and he got it, but still didn't want to waste his last day doing fuck all.

'So Jack, there is a way that you can help, come with me to the Police Station after we finish up here and tell them everything you can remember from that day on Jomtien Beach, also if you can share everything you know regarding Chilli, that will certainly work in his favour.'

Jack nodded and ordered an orange juice to go with his fried breakfast.

While there are some who believe Pattaya has a lot of crime in comparison to other seaside resorts around the world, that just isn't the case. In fact, those who visit the West Indies should be far more concerned as figures in popular tourist spots including Jamaica are far higher. Most of the crime committed here is amongst Thais and the majority of foreign deaths are typically a result of suicide and/or drug overdose.

One hour later, the pair were in a back office in Pattaya City Police Station. Because of Frank's connections and history, they bypassed the Pattaya Tourist Police option. Jack told them everything he could remember from that day at Jomtien Beach and then all he knew about Chilli Matthews. Frank was more interested in him than the Thai Police were. In fact, after the lengthy interview, he pressed Jack for more information to the point where he needed to take a break.

'Have you ever had a Thai massage?'

Jack replied in the negative and twenty minutes later, the pair were enjoying a traditional version of the seedier activity that Pattaya is famous for.

Jack made his daily call to Ice who insisted on a FaceTime chat just to ensure that her man wasn't indulging in more nefarious horizontal activities.

'When you come back?'

'Fuck darling, I haven't even left yet'.

Jack chuckled but inwardly he knew that this would be a question he would face many times during the next half a year.

'It won't be easy Jack'.

Jesus, he thought, is this guy a fucking mind reader or what?

In the next booth, Frank advised Jack to put Chilli out of his mind for now and reassured him that if anything should pop up regarding his friend, he would be in touch straight away. They spent the rest of the day having a few beers and relaxing at some of the private clubs that Frank had membership with.

'Frank, cheers mate, I am going to be getting an early taxi tomorrow so I'm heading back now'.

The older man understood the temptation of being alone in Pattaya for the evening, and as he shook hands, he handed over his business card once more.

The name read:

Frank Matthews - Private Investigator.

End of Chapter Six

▲ *Seedy Love? - Photo by Paul Eddie Yates Photography*

Chapter Seven

DELIGHTFUL DEBS

'So, this is the skanky little whore that broke up my fucking marriage?' The blonde lady was poring over Ice's Facebook page and unleashed a stream of phlegm that covered the entire screen of her laptop.

'Doesn't look much, no tits and skin darker than my shit, not exactly an upgrade is she?'

Shaun wasn't really listening, he took another sip of the overproof rum and stared at the floor. He'd been back from Thailand for a week and had spent most of that time at his sister's gaff. The last thing that he needed was a reminder of the place that had left him in pieces. But he still had a strange yearning for his ex-lover and maybe it was time for him to face up to reality.

Was he actually gay or something more perverse? This was 2019 and surely things like this weren't a big issue anymore. The problem being that he was the most homophobic person in the whole of Wallingford and as such, he'd surrounded himself with a crowd who had the same standpoint.

'Yeah, I'd like to fuck this bitch up, no way is she going to take my man away from me!'

Now he was interested.

'What the fuck are you talking about now?'

Debs sneered at her brother and went on.

'I'd like to cut her tiny little tits off, and mess up that smiling face'.

Shaun looked at his sister, this time with an interested look. She was serious and knowing her as well as he did, Ice was definitely going to be in trouble.

Delightful Debs

'Shaun, are you going to spend the rest of your life moping for that freak that nearly ruined your life or do you fancy some good old fashioned revenge?'

He didn't have to be asked twice, he nodded and started to listen as Debs started to reveal her sick and twisted plan.

* * *

'£150 per week for six months…'

Jack's maths were never that good but, for once, he needed to be on the money, quite literally. It was early June by now and he would be starting his new life in just over six months. Right now he couldn't bring himself to tell anyone his future plans. Who the fuck cared, and if they had a problem, well it was theirs to deal with.

He'd recently managed to find a dead-end job that would at least allow him to get some money together. It would be less than four grand but it was better than nothing. The shrimp farm was a world away from the shitty existence he would be enduring over the next half a year.

Working nightshifts as a bloody security guard wasn't what he'd wish on his worst enemy but work was hard to come by thanks to the pricks in parliament who had fucked the economy once more.

At least his parents were allowing him to stay rent free for now. They had a small nest egg he had been promised for when he finally found a house to buy, but he was fairly sure that they hadn't envisaged him pissing off to Thailand. Worst case scenario, he'd have to do some begging and hope for at least a few thousand pounds.

He'd bumped into Debs in the supermarket and she absolutely flipped her lid. He had to walk away after a few minutes because she started throwing cans of soup in his direction, what a mad cunt she had turned out to be. Shaun was there too but he just walked off. Jack had to chuckle when he noticed the tattoo.

Delightful Debs

Jack couldn't get to grips with why Debs was so bloody angry. Perhaps he was lacking in real empathy but for now, he thanked his lucky stars that he'd escaped from that one.

Bizarrely, Ice was also getting on his nerves. Thanks to that marvellous invention, namely social media, she was never more than a few minutes away. Talk about a double-edged sword. She'd message him day and night and demand FaceTime whether he liked it or not. If he didn't pick up, she'd write a Facebook status that more or less said she was suicidal.

'Fucking Hell, what is it with women?'

He was asking nobody in particular but his phone went off again and this time he answered with some pigeon Thai,

'Sawasdee Teerak!'

Ice was smiling so hard that her eyes all but disappeared.

Six months seemed a lot longer than it did yesterday but at least her man was still speaking to her. It was an apparent fact that Thai women are far more possessive than their Western counterparts and Social Media was their absolute God when it came to venting their feelings. Each status update was met with dozens of emoticons depending on the mood of the poster.

The Industry swallowed up hundreds of thousands of young lives every year, so each of these sisters were really rooting for each other. Nobody knows the true statistics but to say maybe five to ten percent actually get to live the dream and escape this mental existence, would be close to the truth. Western men were not the ideal mates not by any means, but they offered security and a way out of the whoring trade that claimed so many lives.

So Ice was damned if she was going to let this one go back to his fiancée, not a fucking chance!

Delightful Debs

To be perfectly honest, she would have preferred to go to the UK than move back upcountry and work the shrimp farm Industry but Jack didn't seem that keen.

One of the things she loved with Jack was the fact that he came across as honest. That was a quality that she valued above wealth and looks. Although Jack wasn't conventionally handsome, he was above average and carried himself in a way that Ice adored. His blue eyes were something she could lose herself in every time and his broad chest was a feature that none of her previous boyfriends could match. Always smelling nice and with excellent manners, he was a keeper that she would never throw back, not ever!

Jack openly admitted that he was broke and also that he would do his best to find some money to invest in the farm. Her uncle wasn't a greedy man but she knew he would need at least 250,000 baht before he signed the business over. That equated to a little over six thousand British pounds and she knew that Jack did not yet have that amount in his bank.

The other quality that she adored in this Englishman was trust. In a country where corruption and bribery were rife, having a partner that you can trust and depend on was like winning the lottery.

Foreigners could neither own land nor businesses in Thailand without a majority Thai stakeholder. That was usually enough to break up any potential marriage before it even got off the ground. She knew dozens of working girls who had been sent a small fortune from their sponsor in Europe or wherever only to squander most of it on a younger Thai man and eventually, they in turn were ripped off. In fact, this type of ménage-a-trois was so common in Thailand that nobody was even surprised any more, except for the poor foreigner who ends up skint and red faced.

No, this wouldn't happen to Ice and her man, he would send the money each month and this would ensure that she stayed away from Pattaya and saved the twenty odd thousand baht until he came over at

Christmas time. Then their life together would begin. The Industry, the bad memories and his bitch of an ex-fiancée could go to hell!

'Sawasdee Teerak!' She responded with a shriek and looked longingly at Jack's face as if nothing else in their world mattered.

The act of sponsoring a Thai sweetheart between visits is fairly standard and, in theory, it is supposed to work as follows:

The foreign lover/partner returns back to their homeland and whilst staying in contact, they also send an agreed amount of money every month/ two weeks to their Thai love interest/playmate. This amount can range from a few thousand baht to much more.

In return for this investment, typically, the agreement is for the working girl or boy to stay away from the bar scene until their lover comes back to see them. This can be either back at their town/village or perhaps they prefer to stay in Pattaya for the duration.

This arrangement can work, but more often than not, the Thai based person decides that life at home is just too damn boring. They either break the agreement off or decide to keep taking the money and go back to the bar scene. Eventually the Buffalo discovers the deceit and the relationship crumbles into a distant memory.

* * *

Ever since he'd been beaten and dragged away from the airport, Chilli had tried his best to be an utter pain in the arse to Sparky and the boys. It started off when they were torturing him for information regarding any family back in the UK. They simply wouldn't believe him when he smiled and replied, 'I don't have anyone, you fucking chinky bastards!' That earned him a thrashing that removed four teeth and a cut on his face that needed stitches.

Then when Sparky did a little digging and asked Johnny back home, he realised that kidnapping Chilli was going to be a thankless task, so he took out his frustration on him. One month into the ordeal, Sparky didn't bother coming to check on him. Instead, a pretty young Thai lady would visit twice a day and did her best to feed him.

But one day, Chilli had a plan. He pretended to be very sick, hoping that they would take him to a hospital where he could re-enact his vanishing act. Sadly, all he got from that was a visit from an off duty nurse and a few of Sparky's henchmen.

After they left, he was trying to get some sleep when he realised that they had left the door open. Although his hands were in manacles, his legs were free. Chilli managed to get as far as the actual front door of the building before being caught.

This plan wasn't great. He got the expected beating but was kicked so hard that his left leg was broken. Then they threw his arse into a basement and left him for a few days. By the time Sparky had bothered to come and check, with that Thai bird in tow, Chilli was in proper agony.

'Farang, why you make a big fucking problem for me?'

'What can I do with you now?'

Chilli grimaced as he replied, 'Well you fucking rice monkey, you could let me go'.

This retort resulted in an elbow to the face that broke his nose. When Sparky stormed off, the Thai girl stayed behind and produced a pillow and blanket along with some rice. For the life of him, Chilli couldn't work out why they just didn't kill him. He'd always been a loner and right now, more than ever, he wished that someone, anyone, gave enough of a shit to come and find him. Back in Wallingford school, some two decades ago, the only one who gave him the time of day was Jack.

But he had fucked off and was seemingly not even bothered. At school Chilli was in the detention class more than anyone. He had never fitted in. Unsure of who had sired him, he wondered why he looked different to every other cunt at school. Bronze skin and an Oriental appearance had been enough for the others to call him 'Chinky' along with some other choice names.

He giggled like a mad man when he faced up to the fact that he was now in the same country that one or both of his parents had come from. He was going to die here and neither parent gave a toss about their son. Why should they? He'd always been a loser.

When he was old enough, he'd spent a few months trying to locate his parents. Those shitehawks who had given him away. The only scrap of information that he could find was their surname, Matthews. Listening to the heavy rain in the distance, he prepared for a very short future before the inevitable took place.

* * *

The man partially to blame for his demise was drowning his own sorrows with his sister and they were starting to plan the downfall of a certain Thai working girl. Shaun knew that Debs was a mad bitch but he had never seen her in this state.

'I want that whore dead and then I'm going after Jack'.

Shaun was only half listening but he was still keen. Partially because Jack had always come up smelling of roses but also because, well, he was just a sick bastard who enjoyed the misery of others, especially when he was the cause of their ire.

'What ever happened to that dirty little bastard, Chilli?'

To be fair, Shaun hadn't even thought about him much since stitching him up at the airport earlier in the year.

'Don't know, why are you asking?'

'I heard that he had been killed, also that you had told the Thai thugs where he was hiding'.

Delightful Debs

'Whatever, the little wanker deserved whatever he got, why do you care, didn't fancy the little rat did you?'

Whilst it was true that Chilli had fucked his sister once on a drunken weekend, she had other ideas.

'Listen, if we are going to screw Jack and his whore over, we need some local muscle, so I reckon you should see if you can speak to some of those rough bastards sooner instead of later'.

She had a point. Shaun made a mental note to speak to Johnny in the morning, but right now, he was a few pints away from drinking himself into oblivion.

* * *

'Bai, ee hah' (Go, you fucking bitch!)

Sparky wasn't a patient man and nobody could accuse him of being a great communicator, but this morning he had zero time for niceties.

The slight Thai female did as she was told and picked up the two purple notes that were on the table. She hated this man more than any other, but money was her God and this fucker certainly had more than his fair share. As she vacated the pig sty of a room, she checked her phone and it had four missing calls. She smiled and wished that Ice was still working the bars in Pattaya instead of waiting in her village for that farang. Nok was hardcore and ever since the Jet-ski mafia guy had summoned her beyond her will to his favourite bar, she had a steady income, for however long that would last.

As the girl slammed the door behind her, Sparky logged onto his Apple Mac and checked his emails. One in particular had caught his eye, it was from Johnny. Despite his poor grasp of the English language, Sparky managed to decipher the message fairly quickly. Google translate was a fucking wonderful tool.

He read the message a few times and decided to roll a joint whilst thinking over the contents. He had been in business with the English man for a few years and they scratched each other's backs. But this request was a little different than the usual.

Johnny was asking him to help commit a crime. Nothing new there but this was new territory. Sparky had broken many laws in Thailand but he had never raped a woman. Okay, maybe a few, but they'd been paid and usually were asking for it. Besides, whores were not good for anything else.

He was ready to call the man to say no until he read one word.

'Ice'

Fuck, that was the girl he had been looking for ever since that farang prick had crashed one of his jet-skis earlier in the year. She had disappeared soon after, but he'd managed to track down her best friend, Nok. Although she was pretty, she wasn't in the same league as Ice and now, well, the little cunt appeared to be back in the picture. Sparky felt sexually aroused at the mere thought of fucking this little flower and had to smoke another joint to douse those feelings.

To sweeten this deal, Johnny said there was money involved and had attached a photo of the person who was brokering the deal.

'Pooying nom yai mahk' (Big breasted lady).

He said out aloud with a wicked grin. She was a white woman with blonde hair and certainly was gifted in the chest department. Wearing a bikini, she hardly had a gym body but was still a good looking woman.

Fucking hell, he thought, today was getting even better. He'd fuck this foreign bitch for starters and then the sensual Ice he'd have for the main course, or would she be dessert? This woman was not a beauty but Sparky craved after white meat and when he thought over the cash involved, kidnap and rape didn't seem that much of a big deal after all.

Delightful Debs

He called Johnny, who was a tad pissed off at being woken up at 4 am, told him he was up for the deal and then laid down on his bed and had a wank over the two very different ladies. Maybe he could team them both? As he hit the money shot, all Sparky could picture was taking the white whore from behind up her fleshy ass as she dined on that sweet Thai pussy of the smaller woman who was tied to the bed. Life was good…so fucking good…

* * *

'Debs, it's Johnny, can you talk?'

She was surprised to hear back quite so soon and, yes, she could certainly talk.

'I've spoken to my man in Thailand and he's agreed in principle to your suggestion, but has a few requests of his own'.

It was as if he was casually discussing a business plan instead of actions that could ruin and most likely end a life.

'It's best if you come over now, can't talk too much on the phone if you know what I mean'.

'Okay, hun, I'm on my way'.

Five minutes later Debs was sat on the plush leather sofa in Johnny's detached house. She'd often wondered what the fuck this man did for a living. He drove a high end car and was flush yet was always hanging around with scum bags. She was going to find out exactly what Johnny Price did for a living. Whether she liked it or not.

'My man in Thailand is a reliable guy but occasionally, let's just say he throws a few curve balls into the air'.

Debs was intrigued and motioned for him to continue.

'Well, he'd like you to fly over to his place for a week and would like to get to know you a little better before he agrees to carry out the deed'.

Debs smiled and looked Johnny directly in the eye.

'He wants to fuck me, yeah?'

Johnny laughed and started grinding away at the largest rock of cocaine she had ever seen, and she'd seen more than her fair share. Nothing was said until they'd both snorted some of Columbia's finest.

'Yep, you are a good looking lady and our man in Thailand is a horny little fucker. Like all men, I suppose'.

This wasn't an issue for Debs as she would do anything to get her 'payback'.

'What's more, it's a free flight and some spending money'.

'What's the catch?'

Debs wasn't stupid.

Johnny sat upright and replied, 'I need you to take a few signed football shirts for him, no drugs or anything dodgy like that'.

Debs smiled and undid her top so her large breasts were on display, and before Johnny could enjoy the full effect of the Charlie, she was already unzipping his trousers.

'I take it that's a yes then?'

But she couldn't reply as her mouth was already working its way up his erect shaft.

* * *

For Jack, the months dragged by and even though he was in touch with Ice, sometimes more than twice a day, he really yearned for her. Was it love or just something to do until a better offer came along? Who knew? But in his entire life so far, nothing had come close to Ice, and he was pretty sure that this was the best he would ever get.

Because of the long shifts, Jack slept a lot when he was home, and the conversations that he had with his parents were few and far between. They

Delightful Debs

seemed oblivious to the fact that he was slaving away for his future and had very little, if any, interest in his fiancée. On the odd occasion that Ice's name was brought up, his Mum would adopt a strange look as if he was discussing an ingrown toenail or something equally foul and disgusting.

The money was starting to accumulate and there was overtime on offer that helped to make the shitter of a job almost worthwhile. He was being more frugal than ever before. He stopped going to the pub, where in the past he would make a nightly visit and add the price of five beers to his tab each time.

He did splurge however, at the jewellers, Jack brought in the silver ring that was discovered in the belly of the fish. He had it polished and engraved with the words 'You are my everything', Every night he looked at the ring and he planned all the ways he might surprise Ice by asking for her hand in marriage. This is what kept him going back to the crap job and made living with his parents bearable - he was going to return to Thailand, and to his true love.

As well as doing his best to learn Thai, for what that was worth, Jack also invested a few quid in some novels that were about Thailand's culture and even a couple that had been written regarding Westerners who had the nerve to fall in love with a bargirl.

The first one was 'a Woman of Bangkok' written by Jack Reynolds. This was set back in the 50's and told the tale of a twenty something Englishman called Reggie Joyce, who had the misfortune to fall head over heels with a Bangkok Tart known as the White Leopard. Although this was an excellent read with plenty of highs and lows, let's just say that the romance ended badly and it wasn't much encouragement for Jack.

The second book of note was written by Stephen Leather and went by the title of 'Private Dancer'. Also, a very good book, however it hardly gave Jack and Ice much hope. But he had learnt some of the pitfalls that lay ahead and he read both novels twice, underlining key passages that stuck in his mind.

He often thought about Chilli and wondered if the poor bastard was even alive. Everywhere he went in Wallingford, he was reminded of Chilli and sometimes pangs of guilt would shake his body because he knew that nobody else on the earth gave two shits for this man. The embassy had written him off already it had seemed. Jack did some investigation, telling them he was trying to find a relative. But each time, he came up blank.

He vowed to take things a little further once he was living in Thailand, but Ice had advised him to let things be.

'The jet-ski man is very bad and will cause us a big problem if you ask him where your friend is.'

Jack knew that Sparky was definitely behind this and the one time he approached Johnny for some advice, he warned him to just forget Chilli and move on. A couple of times he could have sworn that Debs' car was parked outside his parent's gaff but when he opened the door, the vehicle had driven away at some speed. Shaun was spotted every now and then but, by all accounts, he had turned into a proper recluse. It was still hard to fathom why the man had been such a prick to him and, even more so, to poor Chilli. He had little idea that behind the scenes, Debs and Sparky, and to some extent, Johnny were plotting the imminent downfall of his future happiness and much, much, more besides.

Frank stayed in touch every week or so, but whatever trail he may have been following went cold. He was asking a lot regards Chilli's background in Wallingford which Jack found a little odd, to be honest, but he did his best to fill in any gaps.

According to UK law, it's seven years before a missing person can be declared dead, it had only been a number of months so far.

* * *

Delightful Debs

Debs hated flying even for a short distance but this one was an utter bastard. If she'd bothered to check out the flight time, she would have opted for a stop-over, somewhere like Dubai. The seats on the Thai Airways flight were tiny in economy class and after 2 hours, she had already had enough.

Johnny had paid for her seat and for the hotel in Pattaya so at least she wasn't spending her cash on this shit journey. He asked her to carry a few things in her carryon luggage but they just looked like normal football shirts. Sparky was a massive fan of Manchester City or United. She hated that sport, and this was just to sweeten the deal.

After ordering a couple of G&T's Debs started to relax and, being a nosey cow, she started looking around at the passengers. Most of them were older men and, she was convinced, were going there for the whores. One of the Thai stewardesses looked a little like the bitch who took Jack from her so she took an instant dislike to that one.

For the life of her, Debs couldn't see a single thing in these dark skinned woman that could possibly pique a man's interest. Most were short with a boy like figure and even if some had nice skin, their eyes were permanently squinting and they just looked as if they would be shit in bed.

Admiring her breasts during a toilet visit, she would make sure that not only did that skank pay for what she took, Debs would also make Jack realise what he had missed out on. There's no way she would have him back though, unless he begged and, even then, she'd make him earn her respect the hard way, whatever that entailed.

'Ladies and Gentlemen, we are preparing to land at Suvarnabhumi Airport, please take your seats'

Debs was surprised how quick the flight had been, because she was so engrossed in scripting Ice's last hours on earth that time had flew by.

'That fucking bitch is dead!' She almost said aloud, as Ice's lookalike wished her a pleasant stay in Thailand.

Delightful Debs

Usually Sparky would have sent a minion to collect any mules from the UK but he had a vested interest in this one. He spotted Debs almost immediately because she had a very tight top on and her large breasts were on display. She almost walked past him as, in her opinion, Thai people all looked the same. He grabbed her arm and his smile completely disarmed her. Good thing, as she was going to let loose with that foul tongue of hers.

'Hi Debs, you look even more beautiful in person'.

He'd been practicing that phrase for the last few days and it had the desired effect.

Debs turned to look at the Thai man and she was pleasantly surprised. He was as tall as her and looked quite fit. His skin was dark and he carried himself in a way that suggested he wasn't someone to be fucked with.

'I'm taking you to my house,' he said with some purpose.

She liked the fact that he was direct and wondered if it was true that Asian men had small cocks. Sparky picked up her suitcase and she followed him through the huge arrivals lounge to the basement where his car was parked.

'Did Johnny give you the football shirts?'

His voice was a little less friendly but his face broke into an attractive smile when she produced the garments.

'How far to your home?'

She was knackered and also felt more than a little horny.

'We'll be there in 90 minutes; do you want to stop for a drink?'

Again, she was surprised at how friendly he was and started to perhaps grasp why Thais were so attractive to people from the UK. They were certainly more attentive, and she wondered if this was transferred into their bedroom behaviour.

Delightful Debs

She wouldn't have to wait long as Sparky was already thinking about how to get this blond bombshell into his bed. He'd fucked a few Russian whores before but they were large and surly ladies who may as well have been asleep, for all of the effort they put into the sex. This one seemed a bit more real and he really wanted to see those great big tits, preferably with his manhood between them.

'Why you hate this girl so much?'

Debs was shocked at the change of tack and hadn't really thought of a model answer.

'Well, she stole my bloke and I want her to pay, really want to fuck her up bad'.

He could sense the fire in her words and replied

'But maybe it's not her fault, she is a working girl and your man maybe needs to be hurt more'.

Debs chuckled.

'Oh, don't worry, I am going to teach that cunt a lesson, but I need to sort that bitch out first'

'You hate all Thai ladies?'

This was a weird question.

'Never met one, why do you ask?'

'Oh, I have a girl that is a naughty one, if you want to hurt her, we can maybe use her for… practice'.

Debs was starting to like this man.

'Sure, I could use a little bit of fun, why not?'

Sparky could feel himself getting erect, he hadn't met such a passionate creature for a long time. He was going to enjoy earning this money, very much.

Delightful Debs

They reached the bright lights of Pattaya in less than 90 minutes, and Debs was impressed by the spectacle.

'I will take you on a tour first'.

Sparky grinned and then nearly crashed his car as he realised Debs was fingering herself in the passenger seat.

'Pull over now and fuck me, Thai man!'

'Holy Buddha!' He thought, as he slammed the brakes on and started getting sticky fingers, despite the fact that there were people walking past, and it was in clear daylight. She was much bigger than the typical lady he would lust after, but those tits, well they were to die for. The windows were soon steaming up and the whole vehicle was moving up and down as Oxfordshire and Pattaya joined in a sexual union for all of 300 seconds.

They both enjoyed a post-coital cigarette on Jomtien beach as Sparky stretched and pointed out the Jet-ski business to his latest flame. Debs was still flushed. It was quick and wasn't the best, but by God, she had arrived in Pattaya with a bang, quite literally.

'So tell me, my Thai man, how exactly are we going to catch this little whore?'

He smiled and gave her a sweaty kiss, but the truth be told, he had no fucking idea…'

* * *

Shaun was still angry because his sister was in Thailand and she hadn't asked him along. He was also a proper fucking mess since the realisation that his girlfriend was actually a man. He'd not come to terms with the fact that he'd had sex with a bloke but was even more annoyed that he still harboured feelings for him/her/whatever.

Terrified of bumping into Gary or his cunt of a friend and the ridicule that would no doubt follow, he rarely left the house. He'd seen Jack a few times, but that twat had ignored him, for the best really. Shaun had never forgiven him for treating him like shit back in school but he figured now that they were even, things could get back to normal.

He also wondered, for the first time, if Chilli was still alive or not? Shit, maybe he was finally developing a conscience after all these years…

He was poring over his Facebook page when a message notification popped up. His heart skipped a beat when he realised it was from Mimi's account! He read the message over and over and was quite shocked as he digested the following words.

'Hi Shaun, I miss you but have big problem, please can you send me money?'

Okay, it wasn't the most romantic content but at least it was something.

'Of course, but what's the problem and how can I send you money sweetheart?' He replied.

Jesus, he was being all lovey dovey with another human who had a penis!

Perhaps he was gay after all?

* * *

Meanwhile one mile away, there was another UK-Thai social media conversation taking place. Each day she asked the same question.

'I miss you Jack, when you come Thailand?'

Even though Jack felt the same way, it killed him to see his fiancée in tears.

'Ice, don't cry love, this is the plan and we agreed that I'd come at Christmas time. I will have money for the shrimp farm and will never leave you again'.

These words had the desired effect, and Ice's features were transformed thanks to that beautiful smile. The months had dragged and it was still another four before they'd be together.

Delightful Debs

After the conversation Ice pondered regarding the secret she had been keeping from her fiancée. She decided he would appreciate it more when he finally arrived, and she went back to helping her mother prepare their late evening meal.

Debs had been in Thailand a few days and was starting to enjoy the way that this place worked. Okay, Pattaya was more like Blackpool than the real Siam but it was a bloody good crack. She laughed as she remembered the incident from last night. Sparky had arranged a little role play that had turned her on like never before.

He was in bed with a Thai girl and Debs had barged in, as planned, and things kicked off. It was almost cathartic as she had dreamt many times of catching Jack and his own whore at it in bed. The girl was genuinely scared and surprised. Debs had pulled her out of the bed and given her a proper beating.

Poor Nok tried to fight back, but Debs was twice her size and almost as strong as a man. She'd kicked Nok in the face whilst she was lying on the floor and bruised her all over, specifically targeting her small breasts and face.

Nok looked at Sparky for help but he was almost as turned on as his white bitch of a friend. Sparky thought it would be a good idea to have a threesome, but Debs threw Nok out of the room naked and bleeding. Then she and Sparky made the most passionate love she had ever known.

She was still grinning when she thought of the expression on that Thai whore's face but for the life of her, Debs couldn't see what any man, let alone her Jack, would find attractive in these boyish skanks. Flat chested, slit eyes and usually no arse to speak of, maybe their prowess in bed made up for that but she seriously doubted it.

Debs spent one evening prowling the bars of the Beach Rd and the little Sois that connected it to the second road and also Soi Buakhow. She marvelled at the pathetic sad losers that populated these watering holes and was amazed when she realised that hardly any of these perverts were interested in her. In fact the only interest she got was from a few of the Thai girls who were obviously lesbians. She did think of taking one back to a short time room but the idea of catching something put her off. One of the male gogo bars caught her eye and after buying a few drinks for a particularly hunky lad, she almost started to understand the appeal.

Less than a week later, Debs was back in dreary Oxfordshire pleased that she'd put the wheels in motion for the demise of Jack and Ice.

End of Chapter Seven

▲ *Time to Relax - Photo by Paul Eddie Yates Photography*

Chapter Eight

CHILLI RETURNS

'Farang, you eat this food or you die!' Chilli had been in this shithole for months now and in his current state, arms bound and legs useless, the only way he could manage the food was to be spoon fed, that was happening, or to roll around on the floor and eventually, his mouth would connect with the shallow bowl of rice that ended up almost anywhere except in his starving guts.

He'd long since given up on being found, mainly because nobody back in Wallingford gave two fucks for him. Shaun had practically handed him over to Sparky's mob and Jack was probably in love with that little Thai bird. Not that he could blame them, Chilli had been a complete selfish prick ever since he could talk and perhaps this was Karma.

Stooping down to pick up the spilt bowl, Nok managed to place a few servings of the rice directly into Chilli's mouth. She was still physically and emotionally sore from the beating meted out by that big white bitch a few weeks earlier. Sparky had overstepped the mark this time and it was not a matter of if but when she was going to leave him. This poor excuse for a human had treated her badly from day one. Whilst it may be true that a lot of Thai men do not respect their wives and girlfriends, even a whore from Pattaya had her limits.

She looked at Chilli with pity in her eyes, he would end up dead or even worse.

Nok's plan was fairly simple, she would wake up early the very next day and pretend to go shopping. Instead, she'd board a bus to Buriram and stay with Ice until she figured out what to do next. She very much doubted if Sparky would come and look for her, if he did, well, she would rather die than return to this way of life. She had heard that there was a decent bar scene in Chiang Mai. Maybe that would be far away enough?

Sparky surveyed the scene and was already thinking of the next time he would be able to have sex with Debs. She was very similar to him and he wondered if there would be scope for them to have a future.

He chuckled and gave Chilli a powerful kick in the head that sent the bowl flying across the room.

'Why you help this farang?'

He yelled at Nok and gave her a backhander that knocked her off her feet. That bitch had served her purpose, he'd already thought of a ruse to lure Ice out of hiding and Nok played no part in that game. He'd most likely kill her in the next few days as she knew way too much and she'd already thought of stitching him up with the police. Yes, tomorrow would probably be her last day.

They drove back to Jomtien in silence, each of them deep in thought.

* * *

'Have you been stealing from me again you sneaky cunt?'

Debs shrieked at her younger brother who was doing his best to avoid any eye contact.

She had noticed the odd twenty-pound note missing, that wasn't a problem, but when her card had disappeared and she discovered that her current account was £300 lighter, enough was enough.

'It was just a loan until my dole money comes through'.

If she'd known that the money was already winging its' way to Pattaya via Western Union, she would have blown a fuse.

Shaun was still smitten with his working boy and he'd decided that he would be going over there as soon as he came up with a plan to get enough money. Their parents were fairly rich and Shaun had noticed some tasty antique jewellery that his mother had not worn for decades. Thanks to one of Wallingford's many specialist shops, he'd already got a quote for that ring with the large gemstone. Over twenty grand was the ball park figure, easily enough for a year in Thailand. When that ran out, well, he could deal with that when the time came.

He'd heard Debs speaking to someone on her phone enough times to realise that she was thinking of a return trip around Christmas time.

* * *

Jack continued working nights, sometimes two weeks without a break, simply because he knew it was the only way to get back to his fiancée. During the months leading up to Christmas, he could feel his connection to Ice getting stronger, he'd starting speaking Thai to her and, as a result, he was becoming fairly adept at this language.

He'd continued reading books on the 'Culture Shock' that was going to be inevitable and even played Thai music around the house, much to the annoyance of his parents. Regards his future career as a shrimp farmer, there was shitloads of videos and forums covering the required skillset.

One week before he was due to fly out, Jack's parents took him out for a meal.

'Are you sure this place is open?'

They were climbing down the steep stairs that led them to the 'Thai Corner' restaurant in Wallingford.

Although the sign on the door clearly indicated it was open, the lights were so dim that they had to use their hands to navigate their way safely to the next level.

'Well I booked a table so I would bloody well hope so!'

Jack replied before using the torch on his phone to look around.

'Sawasdee Ka!'

Chilli returns

The three of them jumped with fright as the high pitched Thai female voice came from nowhere. Then the lights came on and they were faced with an attractive forty-something lady who was smiling from ear to ear, this was accompanied with a traditional Thai wai. Jack immediately bowed back as his parents shuffled their feet awkwardly with shy grins.

Five minutes later the three of them were sat at their table and ordering food.

'I sorry, the lights not on, last night have party and we sleep very late'.

The manager laughed infectiously as she recommended the Thai fish cakes/Tort man pla for the starters.

Jack had booked the table for them two weeks ago, knowing that it would be the last time he saw his parents for a while. To be fair, it had been way too long since the small family had been out together and he was doing his best to make this a nice experience. They had retired a few years back and he watched as they had transformed into an elderly couple in front of his eyes.

They were almost speechless when he ordered their food in passable Thai and the waitress nearly dropped the tray.

'Well son, you are soon going to be with your Thai fiancée, we will miss you'.

He hated the way that his mum would refer to Ice as his 'Thai' fiancée but was so excited for the trip that he didn't bother correcting her.

He vowed never to get in a rut like they had muddled into after retirement. Dad was always in the garden and Mum was obsessed with whatever tripe was being served up on the TV, usually that reality show bollocks. Neither had travelled outside of the UK, unless you count a few trips over the channel to bring back Duty Free cigarettes and booze.

'Well, this is nice'.

His mum was always coming out with this type of drivel, usually when she was feeling nervous or awkward.

'How long did you say you were going for, love?'

Jack sighed and told his mum yet again that he wasn't sure.

The first course was served up and, thankfully, his parents were too busy enjoying the scrumptious fare to ask him any more unnecessary questions. All too soon it was over, and the efficient manager had spirited the empty plates away and the deathly silence returned.

Just as Jack was preparing to ask them what they'd ordered, even though he knew, his phone burst into life and he was relieved to see that, for once, Ice had managed to follow his instructions for this time sensitive call.

'Hello Teerak!'

Her pretty face appeared on his screen and both parents were transfixed

'It's her'.

His mum whispered.

Jack had arranged for this FaceTime call a few days ago when it dawned on him that his parents and his fiancée hadn't spoken to each other yet.

'Hi darling, I am eating food with my parents'

He said in basic Thai

Without waiting for her reply, he handed the device over to his mum and watched her face transform from indifference to delight as Ice worked her magic on both of his parents.

'Hello mama and papa!'

That was enough to get both of them onside.

Chilli returns

What followed was a ten-minute conversation that even included one of the waitresses and the manager as the whole restaurant was very taken by his lovely fiancée.

Long after the call, his mother was on another planet.

'Well, you didn't say she was so lovely, did you?'

'Christ mum, did you think I would marry her if she wasn't?'

Normally she would have replied with harsh words but, for now, Jack's parents were totally smitten with their new potential daughter-in-law. The rest of the night went swimmingly as the restaurant started to fill up with locals.

The only downside was when he returned from the toilets and realised his phone wasn't on the table but the rest of the meal was great and the phone was a small price to pay for his family's blessing.

* * *

Nok had been in hiding for three months when she finally plucked up the courage to visit Ice in her village near Buriram. As she approached the small house, memories of her own childhood came flooding back, overwhelming her. If only her family had been as loving as this one. Abused by her father and uncle and then thrown out by her mother when she finally had the courage to speak about this hideous crime, she'd never returned. This was a tale all too common amongst the working girls who came from poor families in Isaan.

She was a tough cookie, but even she knew that Sparky was just too evil to be fucked with. Nok also had a strong feeling that Ice was in some danger from this man. She'd overheard him and that white slut laughing regarding something they were planning, the names 'Jack' and 'Ice' had been mentioned more than once.

Steeling herself for yet another disappointment, she knocked on the door and held her breath until it was opened. She didn't have to wait long because Ice was there in an instant and greeted her with a wide smile and a warm embrace.

'Nok! Where the hell have you been, my little bird?'

She broke down and sobbed her heart out as Ice sat and listened intently to the nightmare her best friend had been put through.

It was just days from when Jack would fly out but she managed to stay focused on her friend and after introducing her to her family and cooking up a huge meal, the two of them lay side by side on the mattress and talked until the moon was high in the sky.

In the morning, they took the motorbike, in case anyone might be listening, and drove to a remote spot where they could make some sense of what was going on. Ice listened as patiently as she could manage as her friend told her two pieces of information:

1. Jack's friend Chilli was actually still alive and being held captive by Sparky. She had no idea what his intentions were, but they weren't good. The poor man had been subject to beatings and his legs had been broken so badly that it was unlikely he would ever walk again. Ice agreed that Jack needed to be told but she had reservations about the timing. She was scared of Sparky, for good reason and, perhaps selfishly, she didn't want anything to get in the way of her and Jack's future.
2. Sparky was also planning something bad for Ice and this was connected to the woman who had beaten and humiliated Nok three months earlier. She couldn't work out the connection, but warned Ice not to risk meeting him in the future.

Ice was now really worried because she was sure that this gangster would rape and then kill her. She had noticed the way that he looked at her that day on Jomtien beach. She couldn't quite believe that Nok had shacked up with this monster, but at least she was safe now.

'Okay, we go Pattaya tomorrow'. Ice sounded very determined, and instantly Nok started to quiver and tears soon flowed.

Chilli returns

'No sister, we cannot'.

Ice explained about her impending rendezvous on Christmas day and did her best to persuade Nok that all would be well.

'That man, he will kill us both. He will kill your Jack as well'.

This was all that Ice needed to hear to make her mind up.

Okay, he may be a Thai mafia badass but nobody was going to fuck up her future.

If Jack was in danger, then she was going to protect him and remove all obstacles to her ultimate marriage to this wonderful man who she was going to spend the rest of her life with. No way was she going to remain a bar girl and then walk the streets when she was too old for the clubs. She wanted a ring on her finger and Sparky be damned!

'Nok, you can stay with my family but I am going tomorrow'.

Her friend's expression changed from scared to steely determination.

'If you go, I go too!'

That was that, these two young ladies made a pact to do what needed doing, no matter how high the risk.

They discussed a loose plan that centred on the fact that if they could get a friendly policeman to believe their story of Chilli and his whereabouts, surely Sparky's days would be numbered. After all, they were risking their young lives every single time they slept with a man for money and they were still alive. Unfortunately, the odds were already stacked against Ice, because the next few days would show exactly how evil some people can be.

* * *

Debs chuckled with glee as she looked at the battered mobile phone in her hand.

'Like taking candy from a sex pest'.

Sparky had devised a plan to get Ice where they wanted her and the first step was already completed. They'd use Jack's phone to send her a message and instead of her lover, the two of them would be waiting to give her a gory send off. He'd also explained that she would need to install 'Line' which was a social media platform much favoured in Thailand and most of South-East Asia. So long as the sim card was intact and if Ice's number was somewhere in Jack's call history, the rest would be simple. They'd have to wait until Jack was in the air before sending a message and would also be dependent on the fact that Ice was already in Pattaya and not her hometown.

Debs was on it. She used a local toe rag to find out when he was flying out and she laughed when she realised he was due to catch his flight on Christmas Eve, soppy cunt!

She was flying out tomorrow, the 23rd, so plenty of time for them to add the finishing touches.

Shaun was looking so fucking miserable that she decided to enlist his help, he may at least be able to add a little muscle to the event, hopefully.

Sparky had told her that they could get a hotel room somewhere and he'd make sure that nobody would be around to hear the screams and see the carnage that would ensue.

'Debs, thanks so much'.

She wasn't sure if she preferred to see Shaun like this, almost sickeningly nice, or moping around like the stupid fuck nut that he usually was. 'Oh, shut it mate, remember we're not going over there to get your arse fucked. Just be around when I need you okay?'

But Shaun wasn't listening. He'd almost come to terms with the fact that he was travelling for thousands of miles to reunite with that man/woman who had clearly stole his heart. It would be a surprise visit because he wanted the moment to be as special as possible.

Chilli returns

Monday 23rd December 2019

'Debs, are you sure that you've thought this through?' Shaun was only asking because he was now starting to worry for his sister's plan and the possible outcomes. Okay, he'd played a massive part in stitching his ex-friend up but to commit kidnapping and murder as well, that seemed a little bit excessive.

As they checked in at Heathrow, he started to think what would happen in the next few days. He had hoped her fury would have diminished over the months, but if anything, she was even more angry with the ill-fated couple.

Shaun had been wrestling with what was left of his conscience ever since he'd reconnected with his Thai love. He was responsible, at least partly, for the fact that Chilli had disappeared. But he'd also started to worry for Jack and Ice. Perhaps he had softened up since falling back in love?

One look at the snarl on his sister's face was enough to convince him that she wasn't going to back down.

'Oh, fuck off you soppy cunt! Anyway, where did you get the money for this trip?'

If only she knew. Shaun had stolen one of his mum's rings and it fetched a decent price. He was still a sneaky bastard and had no issues with this deceit.

As the plane took off Shaun reflected on the last year and how Thailand had affected the lives of the three men who had flown there together, each with a different plan. There was no doubt that this place had changed all their lives forever.

He wondered how his own story would play out.

For sure, in the next couple of days, one of them would be fucked, if they weren't already.

Jack was the definition of a soft twat, as far as Shaun was concerned, but even he and his Thai whore didn't deserve whatever was in store for them. But at this moment in time, he had to sort himself out and couldn't be arsed to worry about anyone else.

Debs was knocking the vodkas back and was engrossed in some crap movie that was showing on her screen, so Shaun decided to try and get some sleep.

'Wake up droopy bollocks, we're going to land!'

Less than two hours later, they were back in Pattaya City.

* * *

430 kilometres to the North-East, Ice and Nok were boarding the bus for the same destination and the pair of them were as quiet as they'd ever been on this journey. Typically, the two women would be full of chat regarding their trip home and then they'd be looking forward to their next stint as working girls in Sin City.

But this time, well, things were very different indeed. They whispered to each other and finalized the plan as the bus crawled through the Isaan countryside towards the South.

Thai people, being Buddhists, will usually try and avoid confrontation in most, if not all, scenarios. Doing anything to avoid losing face is another trait that this nation holds highly amongst their way of thinking. Neither of these paths were being followed by Nok and Ice. If anything, these young beauties were heading right into a shit storm instead of doing everything possible to avoid one.

'Remember Nok, you need to follow the directions exactly as we decided.'

Nok went over the strategy one more time.

Chilli returns

The plan was fairly basic, as it needed to be:
1. Instead of travelling all the way to Pattaya, they were to disembark at Chonburi bus station. This was a mid-sized city an hour North of the bus's final destination.
2. There they would be met by Ice's cousin and spend the night at her apartment. Somewhere, hopefully, where Sparky couldn't find them.
3. Nok would then meet Jack when his plane landed, and take him to Pattaya.
4. Ice wanted to go to the airport badly, but they decided that she needed to go to Pattaya immediately and talk to as many friends as she could find, and gather their help. After all, she was the star of Porn bar no. 5. She had lain with many men, (and a few ladies), who wielded power in this city. And she had done plenty of favours for others. They owed her, and she was coming to collect.
5. Through her contacts, they would engage the police, and alert them to Chilli's location, and Sparky's wicked ways.
6. Hopefully Sparky would be caught swiftly and be brought to justice.
7. As for the blonde bitch, that was something yet to be determined. The punishment would fit the crime.

The problem with this type of plan was that each part was dependent on the previous one. If that went tits up, the whole thing would collapse.

As for plan B, well, there wasn't one….

Six hours later the pair of them were in the outskirts of Chonburi, safely tucked away in a tiny apartment housing four other young ladies. Ice was asleep before her head hit the straw mattress and her head was full of dreamy thoughts that involved Jack and nobody else.

End of Chapter Eight

▲ *Off to the shops - Photo by Paul Eddie Yates Photography*

Chapter Nine

CHRISTMAS EVE

Shaun had decided to swerve his sister's reunion with Sparky and, instead, had checked back into the very same hotel he'd been staying when he'd met Mimi back in April.

He had little interest in reuniting with that piece of shit Thai fellow, because he not only felt guilty for grassing Chilli up, after all of these months, but he also didn't want any connection with the shit that was going to be done with Jack and his bitch. But the main reason was that he was properly infatuated with Mimi and couldn't wait any longer before finding her/him.

Once checking into the hotel, he had a quick shower, wolfed down some Pad Thai, and stepped out back into the halcyon world of Pattaya and it's thousand odd bars.

It was bloody warm and he was soon sweating more than he would have liked. Instead of opting for the shorts and t-shirt, Shaun was wearing smart trousers, a dress shirt and his best shoes. This made him stand out amongst the rank and file because he wanted to make a good impression. He aimed to sweep Mimi off her feet and he'd even shaved his balls just in case they were called into action. He walked past a few of the Ladyboy bars but pretty soon, he was back at the place where they first met.

Pushing his way through the thick curtains, Shaun hurried to the nearest seat and ordered a Leo beer. The creature serving him looked as if she'd seen better days but still had the cheek to ask for a lady(boy) drink. Shaun refused and after necking the contents, ordered another before plucking up the courage to ask for Mimi.

The ugly server soon realised that Shaun wasn't here for the show and hurried off to see if she could locate her. After a few minutes she returned with a proper smug look on her face.

'She not here, she go with customer'.

Shaun felt a terrible pang of jealousy shoot through his body as he took on the new information. He asked if the server might know where they had gone.

'Mimi go customer hotel for boom-boom'.

'Fucking hell,' thought Shaun, I fly halfway across the globe and I'm still being shat on.

'Maybe they come back here later?' This was offered as a parting shot as the server scuttled off to look for another victim and Shaun was left there, wondering what the fuck he would do next.

After two more beers, he went for a wander and up towards the Beach Road. Less than 200 yards up the road, towards the Walking Street end, he saw a sight that stopped him dead in his tracks. Right in front of the Pattaya Beer Garden complex, in front of dozens of passers-by, Mimi was wrapped around a huge man, who looked at least 60 years old.

By the way he was dressed, Shaun guessed this was a German sex pest, complete with sandals, socks, mullet and a huge moustache. The very thought of this creature pawing at his Mimi made him absolutely sick to the stomach.

They were kissing each other in the middle of the pavement and seemingly oblivious to the rest of the world.

'Mimi, what the fuck are you doing?', Shaun screamed at the top of his lungs as he approached the unlikely lovebirds.

Wearing a tiny skirt and an even smaller boob tube, showing those lovely silicone orbs, Shaun had to admit that Mimi never looked better. Mimi broke away from Herr Giant Haystacks and looked genuinely surprised.

'Shaun honey, what you do here?'

Christmas Eve

Just as Shaun was going to reply, the moustached mountain grabbed Mimi's arse hard enough for the ladyboy to let rip with a blood curdling scream. That was enough for Shaun. He launched himself at the larger man and managed to get his left arm around that massive throat with enough momentum for the both of them to hit the uneven pavement. Landing on top of the huge oaf was a blessing and Shaun, to his credit, started raining down haymakers in front of a shocked crowd, made up of tourists, ladyboys and bar girls.

But his huge opponent in love was dazed but not out, he started to shift his massive frame and Shaun could feel himself being lifted off the pavement. It was time to get serious and he grabbed an empty beer bottle to take this fight to the next level. As Shaun was going to smash it into the German's face, he felt a sharp pain from his skull and warm liquid running into his eyes. Losing consciousness, the smaller man slumped into a jelly like form and was tossed aside like a rag doll. By the time he recovered from the surprise blow, the interrupted lovebirds had fled the scene.

'The Ladyboy, she hit you with her shoe, very hard, you want to go hospital?'

He looked up to a sea of smirks and indifference. They'd seen this type of spectacle so often; it wasn't even back page news anymore.

Nursing his head and finding a stool to sit on, Shaun was forced to face facts. Mimi had sided with the fat fucker and had almost staved his head in with one of those stilettos.

The bar girl who was patiently dabbing the remaining blood from Shaun's face whilst making weird cooing noises had even got the whole event on her phone. No doubt this would soon be on YouTube for all the world to enjoy. 'Fuck,' he thought, this would be connected to the first load of Ladyboy crap that was Wallingford news all of those months back.

The part of the grisly movie that he couldn't quite come to terms with was the look on Mimi's face as she smashed that shoe into the back of his head, not once but two times. In fact, she had to be pulled off by the surrounding throng, Mimi was trying to kill him.

So much for the reunion of the year, sitting at the bar for another hour, necking a half bottle of whiskey, for Shaun, the penny was just going to drop. He meant absolutely fuck all to Mimi, never would. Sobbing his heart out and being consoled by the friendly bar girl, Shaun had hit rock bottom.

During the course of many people's lives, they find themselves on a road to self-destruction. Thankfully, a good number manage to avoid that destination. Be this by luck or just a series of events, things eventually even out and normal service is resumed. Unfortunately for some, like Shaun, the future has been mapped out and eventually they have to make a choice to live or die.

Less than thirty minutes later, on the balcony of his hotel room, on the 13th floor, Shaun had decided. Climbing over the safety rails, looking across the hauntingly beautiful view of Pattaya Bay and surrounding roads, Shaun said a silent goodbye to nobody in particular and prepared himself to leave this world.

* * *

Ten minutes earlier, some 60 odd kilometres to the North, Nok, against her friend's wishes, fired out a text message to Jack on her friend's phone.

Call it fate or just bloody luck, but the contents of that message meant that Shaun had one more shot at staying alive.

Just preparing to launch himself over the side, Shaun was set for a bit of balcony diving when his phone started to buzz in his trouser pocket.

'Perhaps it's Mimi, maybe she does love me'.

Those desperate and frankly unlikely thoughts were the sole reason why Shaun climbed back down and pulled his smartphone free.

* * *

Jack looked at his new phone and just as he was approaching the check-in desk, he noticed a message from Ice.

'Jack, I know where Chilli is and he is still alive!'

'Fucking Hell!' he cursed aloud, much to the horror of the Thai airways desk attendant.

Was Chilli really still on this planet? Why didn't Ice call him with this news and why wasn't she picking up his call? He was at least sixteen hours away from being there and really needed to learn more right now.

Jack knew that Shaun was possibly in Pattaya already, he'd heard as much through the grapevine. He also learnt that Debs was there as well, but for the life of him he couldn't work out why. There was nothing for it, biting the bullet he called his ex-buddy and steeled himself for the difficult conversation ahead. The Facebook call was punched in and he didn't have to wait too long before Shaun answered.

'Oh, it's you…'

Jack was almost relieved to hear Shaun's voice.

'Shaun, I know where Chilli is!'

On hearing these words, Shaun felt a shiver go down his spine.

'You fucking what?'

Climbing down off the balcony wall, Shaun walked slowly back into his bedroom and lay on the bed, sobbing. He listened as Jack explained about the message and started asking him for help. To be fair, he didn't have to ask long because one of the reasons Shaun felt so utterly shit right now was the fact that he was responsible for that reckless cunt's situation.

'I was ready to kill myself'

Jack was too busy talking about Chilli to really take these words in, at least for now.

By the end of the short conversation, Shaun had decided to put his balcony jump on hold, for at least as long as it took to find Chilli. Four hours later Shaun was fast asleep, thanks to a few Valium and Jack was winging his way to South-East Asia, head full of thoughts and heart and loins yearning for Ice.

'Did Shaun really say he was going to kill himself?' He wondered as he started to doze off.

Although it is said that figures are grossly exaggerated, Pattaya has earned the reputation of being the 'Suicide capital of Asia' It is said that every week, if not more often, a foreign tourist jumps to his death from the balcony of one of the many high rise hotels or condos. Sometimes, it has been said that lovestruck 'two week millionaires' run out of money and simply cannot face returning to the dull reality that waits for them back home/ On other occasions, individuals have simply had enough of that life, that they travel to Pattaya to enjoy their last days or weeks drinking with gorgeous ladies before ending it all.

One reported case earlier this year, 2019, described a situation whereby a British man threw himself to his death from the top floor of the Central Department Store, hitting the ground floor of this Mall, narrowly missing shoppers and passers-by. Another British man decided to blow his brains out in a popular Pattaya shooting range, nobody knows the exact reason but thoughts and sympathy go to the family he left behind.

End of Chapter Nine

▲ *The best Chef in Town - Photo by Paul Eddie Yates Photography*

Chapter Ten

CHRISTMAS DAY

Debs woke up in Sparky's bed and the pair of them shared breakfast as the bright sun entered his studio apartment. 'Merry fucking Christmas' she wished him and pulled the Thai man underneath her as she gave him an early present.

Sparky was happy enough to play horse to her cowboy, but his mind was starting to wander. After all, she had already paid him the agreed fee and he was starting to become a little bored of her pushy ways. Today was the day he finally got to fuck Ice; he'd waited almost a year for this.

He tried to put the possible murder and kidnapping out of his mind. Like most psychopaths, he was able to justify almost any crime or violent act.

With Jack's old phone in her hand and the Line application freshly installed, Debs typed in the message that she and Sparky had devised the previous night:

Hi darling, I took an early flight and I am already in Thailand.

Come to meet me in Pattaya. I have a room in Seaview Hotel in Soi 10.

Please be there at midday for a big surprise.

Love, Jack

She hit the send button and the pair of them lay back in the bed for another helping of Christmas 'breakfast'. Debs felt even more horny than usual when something evil was on the horizon. She glanced at the clock on the badly painted wall, it was only 6am, they had plenty of time to get everything just right.

Christmas Day

The phone beeped and Sparky grabbed it first. His face broke into a scary grin as he handed it over to Debs. She also smiled as she read the words out aloud in a mock Thai accent, *'Okay Teerak, see you then xxxxx'.*

The bait had been taken.

* * *

Ice's face broke into a frown as she wondered why Jack had started using Line and why he caught an earlier flight. But after a few moments, she broke out in a huge smile and started rummaging through her bags for the perfect outfit to wear, and she planted herself in front of the mirror with her makeup to make herself even more beautiful.

"Jack, I'm on my way.' She said to her reflection.

Ice completely forgot about the plan, and that Nok was en-route to the airport. The reality of Sparky's threats and Chilli's imprisonment lay by the wayside. The blonde bitch was forgotten.

All she could think of was the look on Jack's face when he saw her.

* * *

Meanwhile at Suvarnabhumi airport, Jack was just making his way through the Thai customs channels and preparing to see Ice again. Except this time, it would be for good. He walked into the arrivals area and was met with the usual sea of faces, both Thai and European.

Looking into the waiting crowd, he looked in vain for Ice, but, after 5 minutes, it was fairly obvious that she wasn't there. 'Fucking Hell, where is she?' He was more concerned than angry, he started calling her on Facebook Messenger but there was no reply.

This was a pisser.

He was just going to try again when there was a tap on his shoulder. Spinning round, he half expected to see her beautiful face but was disappointed to see another Thai lady smiling at him.

'Jack?' She asked almost quizzically.

'Yes?'

He recognised her after a few seconds, it was Ice's friend, Nok.

'Hello love, where is Ice?'

She took his hand and led him to some nearby seats.

Jack started to get worried, why wasn't she here? Had she changed her mind?

Before he could form the words, Nok started to talk.

'Listen Jack, it was me that messaged you about your friend. Ice isn't here, she went on ahead to Pattaya to organize a rescue for Chilli'.

She went on to explain what had happened to him and how she, at first, had helped Sparky care for Chilli.

He was shocked to hear regarding the Blonde lady who attacked her with Sparky and how Nok thought that Ice was in danger. 'So where the fuck is Ice now?'

Nok didn't know exactly.

'She going Pattaya to get help from friends and Mamasan, so we no have more danger'.

She called Ice's phone but no answer. She then sent a Line message. The cell phone reception wasn't always reliable. Was Ice out of range?

After a minute there was a reply. 'I am on my way to Pattaya'.

Nok looked at Jack and said, 'We go Pattaya now!'

They grabbed an airport taxi and both took turns in calling Ice's phone but the fact that she wasn't answering alarmed the pair.

Meanwhile, just leaving Chonburi en-route for Pattaya, Ice placed her phone, complete with flat battery, into her handbag as she went to meet her English fiancée for a glorious reunion in that posh hotel.

Christmas Day

He really did think of everything!

Frank received Jack's text and agreed to meet him in downtown South Pattaya. He'd spent a lot of time trying to find Chilli and had all but given up.

When the taxi arrived and Jack piled out with Nok, Frank was a little confused but was also used to things going topsy-turvy here in Thailand. 'Organised Chaos' was an excellent way of describing it.

Within minutes Nok had filled in the gaps for Frank and just before they headed off, Jack got a text from Shaun who was with them 20 minutes later.

'What the fuck is he doing here?', demanded Frank. It looked as if the two men would square off.

'You absolute cunt, you stitched me right up with this fucking tattoo!' Shaun was seething.

'Well, it's just the truth – you do love cock, yes?'

Frank was teasing him and Shaun was just going to throw a punch when Frank sidestepped the younger man and swept him to the floor with a low kick.

Before the fight could continue, Jack stepped between the two men and said, 'Ok lads, please leave this shit until later. We are here for Chilli and then I need to find Ice, wherever she is'.

This had the desired effect, as they both put their differences aside and decided what to do next.

* * *

It had been a few days since Chilli had eaten and the last drops of water were just a memory on his parched lips. He crawled across the small room and wondered how many days he had left on earth?

There were moans from upstairs and by now, he was fairly used to them. Sometime ago he had figured out that he was being held prisoner in a whore house. He often chuckled to himself as he thought how appropriate it would be for him to end his days in such a low end place.

On occasion he wondered if Jack and that wanker Shaun even cared if he was still alive or not. For sure, nobody else would shed a fucking tear the day Chilli Mathews shuffled off this mortal coil. He'd burn in hell, that was a no brainer. Closing his eyes, for hopefully the last time, Chilli lay down on the floor and switched off.

* * *

Enjoying a late morning beer on the roof of the Seaview Hotel, Debs was tingling with excitement. According to Jack's old phone, Ice was less than 30 minutes away from meeting her fate.

Sparky had hired the penthouse suite and this fairly plush apartment had two bedrooms and a large lounge. They'd left a card key for Ice in reception and once she'd let herself in, Sparky would be waiting in the main bedroom.

Once she was inside, he would overpower the small Thai lady and rape her whilst Debs watched and jeered him on. Once that had ended, Debs would grab her by the hair and dish out the beating of her life. After that, well Sparky could have her again until they were bored of the game.

At that point in time, his cronies would appear and, once her life was snuffed out, they could drop her down the garbage chute and the body would be disposed of. After that, they'd see to Jack…

Ice arrived in Pattaya at 10:30am, and before going to the hotel, she stopped in the Big C supermarket on the second road to buy some of the fruit that she and Jack enjoyed eating together in bed. Rose apples look more like pears than their namesake and the flesh was crunchy and delicious. Although prices in Pattaya were higher than the rest of Thailand, fruit was still a fraction of the price of that in Europe still.

Christmas Day

Hopping on a motorcycle taxi, she arrived at the hotel at exactly midday. Ice laughed as she thought of the way Jack had always moaned that Thai people were always late.

'There's real time and there's Ice time'.

She said this aloud, mimicking his English accent as accurately as possible with a tingle in her nether regions as she imagined the amazing sex she was going to share with her lovely Jack.

She wondered how he would react to her secret?

The room key was waiting for her at reception, just as Jack had said it would be. Ice was soon sliding the card into the door lock device and looked around the dimly lit room. Carefully placing the bag of fruit on the nearby table, she called out his name and turned on the hallway light.

Remembering that her phone battery had died, Ice removed the charger from her overnight bag and carefully plugged in the device. She waited a minute until it burst into life and decided to set the camera to record so that they could remember this precious moment forever. It was still unclear why he hadn't stuck to the original plan, but she would make sure that this hotel room would be the place they started their new lives together.

There were noises coming from one of the doors, walking slowly towards the room, her heart started to flutter

'Jack, are you there my Teerak?'

Pushing the door open she scanned the room before stepping inside.

This was a lovely room with a huge bed…

As she looked across the large bedroom, she walked towards what appeared to be the bathroom and was opening the second door when she heard a voice behind her that almost dropped her to her knees

'Ice, Ice, Ice!'

The heavily accented voice carried a tone of disdain and it was as if one of her teachers from Mathayom three had been reincarnated and was, yet again, disapproving of her actions.

Except the reality was way fucking worse.

She saw the Mafia hoodlum in the mirror moving towards her and she was rooted to the spot with a mixture of disbelief and fear. Ice knew of Sparky's violent reputation and had always kept her distance, until now. Moments later she was thrown to the floor and as her head smashed into the solid teak of the King size bed frame, she could taste the blood in her mouth. Both legs were restrained, and the naked form of Sparky bore down onto her.

* * *

Before they set off, Jack pulled Shaun to one side and whispered,

'What was that you were saying about you were going to kill yourself?'

'Ah don't remind me Jack; I had a shite night but things are much clearer now. Anyway, where's your bird, don't tell me you've traded her in for this one?'

Shaun giggled as he pointed towards Nok who was frantically trying to reach her best friend on her phone. Jack was still knackered from the flight but he knew something wasn't right.

'Nok, where the fuck is Ice?'

She shot him a worried glance and continued fiddling with the mobile device.

'Never mind her, mate, she's eating or something, you know what these birds are like, let's see if we can find Chilli!' Said Shaun.

Jack was sorely tempted to say something along the lines of 'Oh now you give a fuck…' But right now, he didn't have time, there would be plenty of that later. They both looked at Nok with searching eyes. It was as if a choice had to be made, and time could be running out.

Christmas Day

'Chilli near Bali Hai Pier'.

Bali Hai pier is at the South end of Pattaya and is where many of the ferry boats are anchored down when not in use.

After a brief discussion it was decided that as Ice would return the call eventually and, as they'd already checked her old room and spoken to a few of her friends to keep a lookout, they needed to find Chilli now.

They were there in fifteen minutes. Walking in the searing heat wasn't agreeing with any of them and the tensions started to rise. It's also a very busy place with dozens of excursions to nearby Koh Larn.

'Nok, where is this house?'

She pointed to a small row of townhouses that were a few hundred yards away on the hill that led towards Jomtien beach. Minutes later the trio were inside and had gained access thanks to an open window at the back of the ramshackle building.

'This short time hotel that Sparky owns. Sometimes he bring people here to kill'.

She spoke in a casual tone as if she were discussing the purchase of a packet of cigarettes.

Jack and Shaun looked at each other and it was only then that the danger of this task had hit home.

'Fucking hell, what if he comes back?'

Nok replied, 'He not here now'.

Frank produced a side arm that he clearly was ready to use. Nok knew that if she told Jack the probability was that Ice was already in a lot of danger, that would fuck with his head and both Chilli and Ice would be snuffed out.

All of the doors on the ground floor were open and after a quick inspection Jack started to climb the stairs.

Nok had been trying to reach Ice again and when she hung up she motioned to Jack to stop.

'Chilli not upstairs'.

She then pointed back to the kitchen and they followed her into what seemed was a small larder. She then removed a straw mat and revealed a trap door.

'He down there'.

Jack and Shaun looked in amazement. 'Poor bastard is in the fucking basement'. Both men immediately started pulling on the iron handle for all they were worth. Meanwhile Frank was checking the other rooms and listening out for any movement inside and outside the house.

Nok looked on for 30 seconds without saying a word. After they stopped for a break, she produced a key and inserted it into the obvious hole next to the handle.

'Now you tell us that you have a fucking key'.

'You didn't ask'.

Shaun was still a stranger to the Thai ways.

She had the foresight to get a copy made, back when she started to realise that she meant nothing to Sparky.

Lifting the door up with ease, all three looked at each other with different expressions before instinctively holding their noses.

'Oh my God, has something died down there?' Jack said without thinking...

Shaun almost gagged as he tried to clear his head for the task ahead. The would-be rescuers descended, one by one, and there he was, shackled and unkempt but barely alive.

Chilli Matthews.

Christmas Day

Shaun was the first one to notice the pathetic figure sprawled across the hard and dusty floor.

'Jesus wept, is that you Chilli?'

The three of them crouched down and Jack placed his open had over the prone man's nose and mouth.

'Thank fuck, he's still breathing'

Shaun lifted Chilli's upper body off the floor and was going to pull the smaller man into an upright position until Nok pointed to his legs and shook her head vigorously.

'Look at the state of his bloody legs!'

Jack grimaced and they witnessed the way that both legs appeared to be grossly misshapen between the knee and the feet. It was fairly obvious that they had been broken with some force and without the proper medical treatment they were probably not going to work again.

'He try to escape many time and Sparky was very angry with him so he smash the legs with hammer'.

Nok explained in a frank way that both men were struggling to take on board.

'That slimy cunt, wait until I get hold of him'.

Shaun was talking as if he was a hard man, and Jack soon pointed out,

'Mate, not being harsh but you were the fucker that grassed him up in the first place.'

Shaun looked at both men as if he would burst, but then shut up as he was banged to rights. They did their best to lift the wounded man up and just as they reached the ground floor, Frank motioned for them to be very quiet.

Then the front door opened.

* * *

Ice came to and instantly realised that Sparky was now on top of her and she was very much naked. She instinctively placed her hands on her stomach area to check for any issues and then moved them down to try to stop him entering her.

Suddenly another pair of hands appeared as if from nowhere and she felt a sharp pain as it appeared, she was being strangled. Debs squeezed hard and felt a strange thrill as she had finally met the whore that blew away her impending marriage.

'You fucking slut, where's that smile now hey?'

Sparky was now having his way with Ice and Debs was enjoying the twisted show. She even felt a little horny as she squeezed Ice's small breasts as hard as she could muster. Debs kneeled on Ice's shoulders so she couldn't move, and Sparky alternatively sucked and bit the girl's nipples. The pain was excruciating and Ice wept silently, wondering what she had ever done to warrant this treatment. The poor girl was being raped by this vile couple and there didn't seem to be much that she could do except scream. And scream she certainly did.

'Choi Duay!' (Thai for help me!)

The sheer volume of this stopped Sparky in his tracks, or at least for a moment.

'Oh you little bitch. You have no idea who you are dealing with', sneered Debs.

'You are not going to make one more sound because I can't stand to hear your weepy

voice. We are giving you everything you deserve and more. And you are going to take it without making a sound, or the punishment will get more severe.' Debs slapped her face and kicked her prone body.

Ice didn't really understand the words being spoken to her, but she was terrified, and couldn't help the whimpers that escaped her mouth.

Christmas Day

'She say no noise', and with those words, Sparky pulled Ice across the rough carpet by her bound legs and dangled her out the window.

'Don't bring her back in until she stops crying', said Debs. 'Then we'll get down to business'.

Ice screamed some more, but no one in the street even looked up her way. Tourists must be used to the commotion of the city, and didn't think it was worth glancing up to see a naked body swinging from an open window. Ice finally realized that the only chance she had of escaping was to stop making noise so she could be brought back inside.

'Finally the whore shuts up', noticed Debs, motioning to bring Ice back into the room.

Sparky dropped Ice roughly onto the floor, removed the ties from around her ankles, and arranged her on her hands and knees.

'No noise', he warned.

He sat in a chair and watched as Debs beat her. Ice didn't make a peep. Watching the two women, the large white one and the tiny dark one, he couldn't help but get aroused again.

'Debs, take off your shirt'.

Sparky decided that he'd get his fantasy one way or another. He watched the blonde remove her clothing, her large breasts were magnificent and he had an idea. He stood up and moved his chair in front of Ice, straddled his legs around her head, and he sat Debs on the whore's back and leaned over to nuzzle those amazing white tits. He would soon have Ice tend to him.

Ice sensed that this may be her only chance to escape, and using all of her might, she pulled free of both of them and aimed a punch at her rapist's testicles. Sparky felt the full force and rolled off the chair in agony.

Ice jumped up, only to be punched in the face by the much larger Debs. It may have been the adrenaline or maybe the will to live, but Ice hardly felt the blow and pushed past her attacker whilst Sparky was still trying to get up.

'You useless cunt, she's getting away!'

Debs screamed as Ice was running towards the door, still naked.

Sensing that she just needed to open the door to get to freedom, Ice grabbed her phone had almost reached the handle when Debs grabbed her hair and pulled her in the opposite direction.

'Who the fuck are you, bitch?'

She screamed in Debs face.

'I'm the woman whose husband you stole, you filthy whore!'

The two women faced each other and Ice then realised who she was dealing with. Ice had been in many rough situations, both paid and unpaid, which is not unusual for a bar girl. But she had never feared for her life as much as in this moment.

Holding a beer bottle and eyes ablaze with pure hatred, this white woman was a scary sight. It was Jack's ex, and Ice knew that she had to act now if she was to see him ever again.

Tempting as it was, she didn't bother continuing the conversation as she dropped down into a stoop, like her Muay Thai trainer had taught her over ten years ago.

Debs was a little confused by this change of stance and took a half step forward and placed her arms around Ice as if to pull her in for a hug. Her face was then met with Ice's knee as the Thai girl brought it up with full force, smashing her nose and many teeth in the process.

Debs was out for the count and Sparky was still trying to get his wind back.

Ice had enough time to pull on her shorts and top and sprinted out of the room with her phone, leaving just the rose apples and would-be murderers back in the room. Instead of using the lift, Ice opted to use the stairs and a minute later, totally breathless, she ran through the reception and into the busy Soi.

* * *

Somboon was having a shit day, he'd been driving passengers all around this shitty town and was bursting for a piss. His next fare was on the beach road in 20 minutes so he decided to cut through Soi 10 and stop at the small restaurant owned by his uncle.

It was around one-thirty pm and as he pulled into the small road, he cursed his luck as he had to slow down for a somtam cart. The old lady was taking her sweet time and as she finally pushed the contraption to the side of the road.

'E hah' (Thai slang for bitch), He muttered and pressed the pedal to the metal as the urine was starting to work its way through his groin.

He looked down to ensure his wallet was still in the centre console and as he looked up, he saw a figure in the road, literally feet away from the front of his Toyota. Somboon slammed on the brakes but it was too late.

Ice's body was hurled into the air and somehow, she managed to land on her feet, like a human cat, but then she slowly crumpled into a bleeding heap on the ground. Her phone hit the road a few seconds later and Somboon pulled over as his own piss drenched his trousers.

* * *

Back in Bali Hai, Frank motioned for Chilli and his would be rescue squad to stay still and not move whilst he removed the safety catch from his pistol.

Seconds later, two Thai men entered the building and by the way they were walking, they were both pissed as farts. They seemed distracted and by the sounds of it, there were a couple of ladies in tow. Both men clumsily started walking up the stairs and ten seconds later, two scantily clad Thai females followed suit. The first one clambered up the stairs but the second seemed a little distracted.

'Chan ben uak', She muttered, meaning she was feeling sick. She ignored her companions and started looking for a toilet instead. This brought her into the kitchen where she was faced with the hapless foursome.

Just before she screamed, Frank came up behind her and, with some ease, choked her out. Jack was surprised by the speed of the older man but grateful, nonetheless.

Frank looked up, 'Okay we don't have time for any more shit, let's leave now.'

The others didn't need any more encouragement and they followed him out of the open door.

'Fuck me that was close, Frank where did you learn that shit?'

Shaun was still in shock at the way that Frank had moved earlier.

Instead of replying to him, Frank started barking out instructions.

'We need to split up, Shaun and Nok, can you take Chilli to the hospital, Jack come with me'

Jack responded, 'But what about Ice?'

Frank looked back at him and replied.

It's most likely that Sparky is with her now'.

Jack didn't want to hear this but knew that Frank was their only chance now.

Then, as if by cue, Nok's phone burst into life. After less than ten seconds Nok looked directly at Jack and said one word that shook his world.

'Ice'.

Christmas Day

She explained, through tears, that it was the hospital and that she had been admitted less than 20 minutes earlier.

'But what the fuck happened?' Jack was fighting back his own tears by now.

'She have accident'.

He fucking hated that word and the way Thais used it to describe almost every incident that had gone tits up.

'We go now!'

They piled into a Taxi and were in Pattaya Memorial hospital 15 minutes later.

Thanks to Nok, they quickly located the doctor who called her mobile and, judging by his grim expression, the news wasn't good.

'The lady, she very injured because the car hit her and she lost much blood'.

This wasn't going down well with Jack.

'What the fuck happened to Ice?' He yelled at the doctor who was having a shit day so far.

'Sir, please calm down, she is in theatre now and we don't know why this happened to her'.

Handing her battered phone over to Nok, he explained that she was barely conscious when admitted but managed to ask them to call Nok as soon as possible, which they did.

They found some seats and the waiting began.

'Nok, can I see her phone please?' Jack almost pleaded, and Nok, seeing the pain in his eyes, she handed the device over to him.

Shaun was also checking his phone and was trying to contact someone.

'Who are you calling?' Jack noticed that his friend's expression had changed to a guilty one and sensed that he hadn't been entirely honest.

Facing Jack with a lot of regret in his eyes, Shaun started to speak,.

'Mate, it's Debs, she came over with me and I think she is behind this whole fucking mess'.

He went on to explain about his sister's revenge mission and once Sparky's name came into the picture, Jack started to feel his blood boil.

'Why the fuck didn't you tell me before?'

Shaun had no answer but Jack had already started looking into Ice's phone, hoping for a clue.

Nok approached the hospital staff and managed to get a few titbits of information. The taxi driver had scooped the injured lady into his arms and had delivered her to the hospital, shit, he'd even called the local police and gave himself in.

According to the staff nurse who was on duty when Ice arrived, the accident happened in Soi 10 outside a large hotel. She'd ran into the road and the driver had no chance to stop in time.

As she walked back to where Jack and Shaun were sat, she noticed a policeman walking the other way and had asked him to come and help them. Frank knew this guy and they started having a conversation in Thai.

Meanwhile as Jack was browsing through the history of Ice's phone, he noticed that there was a large video file that had been saved that day, less than an hour earlier. Pressing play, he and Shaun watched as the mini movie spluttered into life on the cracked screen .

The contents played out something like this:

There was a small table and it was laden with a variety of fruit; Jack recognised the rose apples and felt a warmth that reminded him just how much this woman cared for him. The figure of a woman, Ice, was then walking towards a door. Even though it was dark, they could see that once she entered the room, there was another person appearing from the other doorway.

'Debs!' They both exclaimed as the video went on

There was a commotion in the first room and when Sparky's naked shape appeared, they both shouted out aloud

'Look out Ice!'

Of course, it was no use…

The man struck her and then her head connected with the corner of the bed frame as she fell on the floor.

At this point, Debs entered the room and both men were transfixed as they watched the video in silence.

He appeared to pin her down and then Debs was getting involved. She started hitting Ice with both fists.

The point where Ice was taken to the window was almost too much for Jack to take in and when she was then thrown to the hard floor in the room, he was ready to scream out in anger. Sparky then instructed Debs to beat Ice and after ten seconds, it seemed as if he was trying out a perverse act for his own amusement.

Suddenly things slowed right down and Sparky tumbled off the bed, Ice ran out from the room but was pulled back by Debs who had something in her hand

Jack couldn't bear to watch but before he could press the stop button they both looked in amazement as the much smaller girl smashed her knee into Debs face.

'You fucking go girl!'

Jack whispered and then, after twenty seconds, the video clip ended.

The timestamp showed that this all took place around midday.

Christmas Day

Frank then took the phone and watched it himself.

They left him and Jack played the video over at least five more times, wondering why the fuck Debs was there and if he would ever see Ice again'.

'Okay, we can't do anything here, let's see if we can find Sparky and Debs before they leave Pattaya'. Frank was making sense, as usual.

What seemed like hours later, after a lot of activity around the ward where Ice was being operated on, Jack was aware of the same surgeon, this time in a blood-stained tunic, standing before him with an earnest look on his face.

'Jack, are you the lady's fiancé?'

'Yes I am, what's going on?'

The surgeon beckoned for Jack to follow and they walked together, through the double doors until they reached a bed that was surrounded by a fame of curtains.

'She is dying, I am sorry'

Jack started weeping as the doctor continued. 'She lost too much blood, because of her condition, we couldn't operate quickly enough on the vital organs'

'What fucking condition?' Jack screamed and pushed past the man through the curtains, and there she was.

Her once bronze and vibrant skin was replaced with a grey sheen and, judging by the number of tubes connected to her, Ice was fading fast.

Jack was filled with a mixture of terrible sadness and an uncontrollable rage. One thing was for sure, those fuckers would pay for this. He stepped forward and instinctively held her hands, despite the surgeon's shaking head.

'Oh my poor darling, what have they done to you?'

Christmas Day

He squeezed gently as the tears were streaming down his face and onto her arms.

She felt warm.

He looked at the surgeon with a quizzable look.

'Jack, she is not here for long now'.

Suddenly her eyes opened and the faintest glimpse of a smile appeared on her face.

'Hello Blue Eyes'

It was clear that she was struggling for breath.

'Please…I am sorry'

This wasn't what he wanted to hear.

'Ice my darling, I promise I will kill those bastards'.

But she interrupted him. 'Remember, I love you. Family first. 'We have…'

'You are my family', Jack replied. 'You are my love and my soulmate. He took her limp hand and slid the shiny, engraved catfish ring onto her finger.

'This was supposed to be a symbol of luck for us', he said.

She was trying to move and speak. As she attempted to sit up, it looked as if she was pointing to a door at the back of the room. But it was too much for her. She lay back down and those beautiful almond eyes closed for maybe the very last time.

'No! Don't give up darling…'

Jack could sense the life leaving her body and was in complete shock.

'Jack,' said the doctor in a gentle voice, 'She is gone, I am sorry, we did all we could'.

'Nooooo! Jack's wail could be heard throughout the thick walls of the hospital.

He threw himself onto Ice's body and cried.

'Ice', he whispered, 'You said we would be together forever. You can't leave me now. Come back so we can start our life together as husband and wife. I've worked so hard to get here and I've abandoned all that is familiar to me, to start fresh with you. Come back to me.'

Jack held her hand and lay his head on her chest.

Moments later he bolted up and screamed 'Doctor!'

The physician and nursing staff ran into the room.

'What is it Jack?'

'My hand. She squeezed my hand.'

'Jack, she's passed. This is just a reaction of her nervous system as it shuts down'.

'No. I think I can hear her heartbeat'.

The doctor pushed Jack aside and listened for himself.

'Nurse! Start the IV again and hook her up to the monitors. She has come back to this earth. It is a miracle'.

'This is a day for miracles, isn't it?'

Jack turned around and saw a person in a hospital uniform backing out of the room that

Ice had pointed to earlier. He watched as she turned around and pushed a trolley with a clear box on top towards him.

What he saw next made him fall onto his knees in disbelief.

Helping Jack up to the chair, the surgeon was now smiling as helped the nurse with her trolley. As they approached, he looked down into the box and saw the most beautiful site in the world. It was a perfectly miniature version of Ice.

Christmas Day

Jack stood up and looked straight into the eyes of a newborn baby. He could have sworn that this little being had the same expression that Ice first wore when they met all those months ago.

'Your fiancée gave birth to your daughter before we could operate. She was 8 months pregnant'.

Jack could not speak but as he looked again into those lovely brown eyes, all of the anger slowly left his body. That must have been what she meant by 'Family First…'

She was in an incubator but she looked perfect.

The surgeon was offering him a drink of water but all that Jack could do was to look at his daughter and thank God, Buddha, whoever, that Ice was still here and had given him such an unbelievable gift - an instant family! He was even more thankful that Ice might survive to raise this child with him.

In the background he could hear a Christmas song playing and he looked back at Ice as they wheeled her out of the room and back into surgery.

'I love you, my darling', he whispered through tears and gazed back at their child before slumping back into the chair, exhausted, emotionally drained and utterly overwhelmed by all the day's events.

He was a father now, and needed to sort this out in his mind. He would never leave his girls again. Jack was here to stay.

End of Chapter Ten

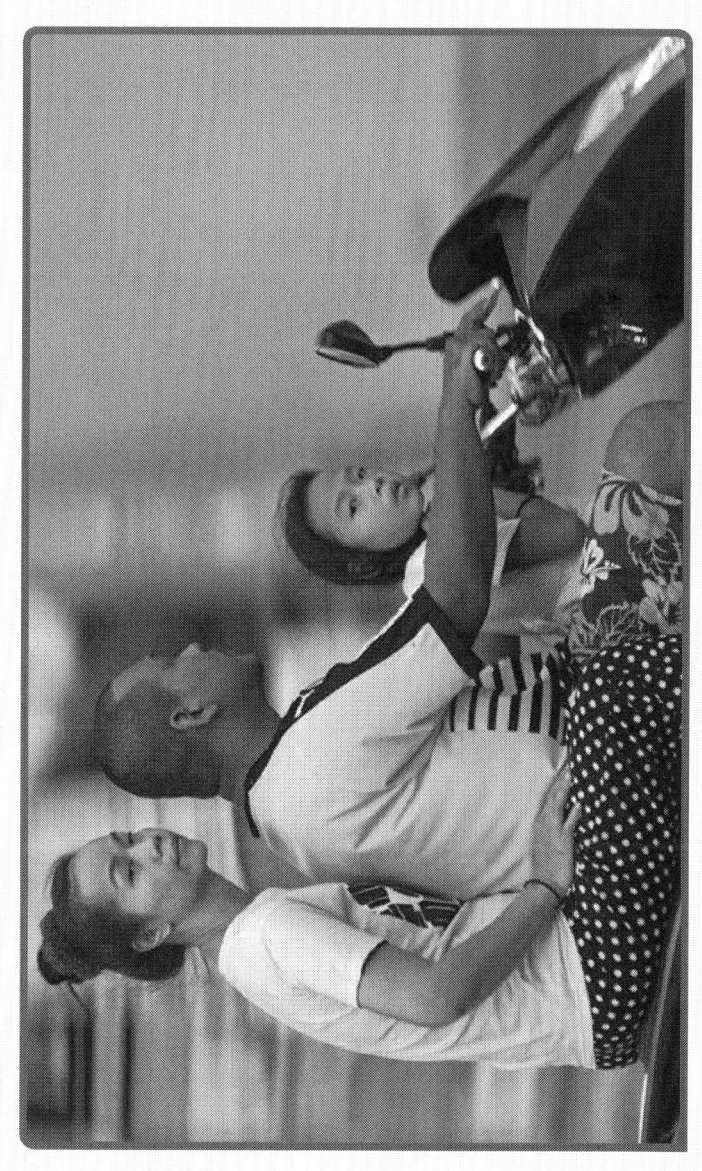

▲ *Eyes Right - Photo by Paul Eddie Yates Photography*

Chapter Eleven

END GAME

F rank made a quick call to his Thai Police friends and when they arrived outside the Soi 10 hotel, they were already waiting. Facing Nok and Shaun, Frank explained, 'Okay, both of you know what the woman looks like, we'll use the police car to search for that pair of cunts. The cops know Sparky so they'll do a sweep of the places where he hangs out'.

Shaun and Nok nodded and a few minutes later, the two cars drove off in different directions. Frank's phone starting ringing as he pulled away so he pressed the hands-free button linking the call to the car's Bluetooth system. The one way conversation was in Thai and very brief. Shaun had no clue what was said but he could guess by the way that Nok started crying that Ice was hanging on by a thread.

Frank's expression changed as he explained to the pair that this case was now being upgraded to attempted murder. Shaun's mind started turning into jelly as he knew that Ice was close to death because of him. As if Frank could sense his distress, he pulled the car over and looked at him saying,

'Shaun, you weren't to know'.

They continued the search but after an hour, the gruesome twosome were nowhere to be found.

'Frank, can we go back to the hospital to check on Jack and Chilli?'

It made good sense and Frank was just ready to take a left when his phone started to ring. This time it was a far more excited voice coming through the speakers. Frank reacted by doing a cheeky U-turn as he gunned the car towards Jomtien Beach.

'They've been spotted!'

The car accelerated up Jomtien Hill, almost clipping a motorcycle as they skidded around the corner. Shaun and Nok were both clinging to the seats. Less than five minutes later, the car reached the spot where two cop cars were waiting.

The three of them got out and Frank approached the waiting Police. After a few words and some pointing, Frank beckoned for Shaun and Nok to come over, handing them a pair of binoculars. They took it in turns to confirm that the couple crouching behind a beach umbrella and some deck chairs were certainly Pattaya's version of Bonnie and Clyde.

Sparky cursed his fucking luck, why had this turned into such a mess? When he saw the Police cars arrive, he knew that things really had gone tits up. Now it seemed that Nok and Shaun were here, as well as that old farang. What did it have to do with him? Looking at the sea and then back at the now approaching Police, he reached for his hand gun and grabbed Debs by the hair, pulling her down to the ground.

'What are you fucking doing?' She started to shout, but he smashed the gun into her temple and crouched down, using her now limp body as a shield.

'I will shoot her if you come closer', he bellowed out in English and then Thai, just in case the Police didn't get his drift.

This had the desired effect. The Police and Frank stopped in their tracks and started talking. Just for the hell of it, Sparky aimed a few shots in their direction. They scrambled for cover with Frank moving to the left, just out of sight.

'Shaun baby, there you are! Where you go?'

Everyone turned to see a tall woman wearing a strapless dress with most of her cleavage hanging over the top. The shimmery dress was hiked high well above her thighs, and she teetered on five-inch stiletto heels, the outfit more appropriate for a Tokyo nightclub than a sandy beach. Mimi was strutting towards her ex waving her arms as she screeched. Shaun saw her and froze, then crouched back down out of Sparky's sight.

'Shaun you naughty boy, I come give you sweet loving. I seeee you'. (See is Thai slang for having sex)

Mimi pushed right past Sparky and tripped over Debs as she made her way to Shaun's hiding place.

'What the Fuck?' Mimi cried as she fell to the ground.

Grateful for the diversion, Debs managed to attack Sparky in an attempt to free herself.

'Fuck this!' said Sparky, and he shot Mimi in cold blood and kicked Debs in the face. He then picked up his hostage and continued on his way to escape the madness.

Fishing through his jeans pockets Sparky found a set of keys that were now his only hope. He dragged Debs' limp body to the shoreline and placed her onto the seat of the nearest Jet-ski. Firing it up he looked back at the beach and was satisfied that his escape route was going to be successful. He would take the vehicle to the nearest water skiing station and from there, he'd take his speedboat up the coast to Sattahip, some 10 miles away. After that? Well he hadn't thought that far ahead but something would come up.

As for Debs, he would toss her body into the water as soon as he was out of range from those Police guns. She had served her purpose and he was bored of her ways already. Great tits but not much else going on. Besides, if the police questioned her, she'd squeal. He revved up the engine and started the mad dash to the podium. It was 300 metres from the shore.

Back on land, Shaun ran to Mimi, and saw the bloody mess that poured out of the gaping wound in his/her head. Mimi was unresponsive, and had no pulse. There was nothing to do but call the paramedics, and the morgue.

Distraught at the loss of Mimi and the abrupt end of his first man-on-shemale relationship, he raced to catch up to Frank who was headed to the fleet of jet-skis that were lining the beach. They each jumped onto one of the wave-runners and hit the water, picking up speed.

Less than a third of the way there, Sparky looked back to see that two of his jet-ski fleet were manned and already approaching. It was Frank and Shaun and, by the looks of it, they were gaining fast! With less than 100 metres to go, both jet-skis were almost drawing level with, possibly because of the combined weight of him and his prone hostage. Without so much as a thought, Sparky then shoved Debs over the side and continued gunning towards his target.

Exchanging glances, Frank fully expected Shaun to slow up and pull his sister out of the water, but Shaun didn't look twice. He was gunning for Sparky and was seeking vengeance.

'Careful, he's got a gun!' He yelled out but Shaun was already out of earshot.

By the time Frank had rescued Debs, who was unconscious and barely breathing, Shaun was already climbing onto the podium. Sparky turned around to see Shaun facing him and as he aimed the pistol at the Englishman's head, he chuckled.

'That tattoo, you know what it means?'

Shaun took a few steps forward and replied, 'Yes and it's true. You just killed my lover and now I'm going to kill you.'

Sparky laughed loudly and aimed a shot just above Shaun's head.

'Okay Faggot, have I got your attention now?'

Shaun started running towards Sparky, despite the fact he was facing down the barrel of the hand gun. Sparky pulled the trigger but instead of a loud bang, the weapon simply emitted a click and not much else. The chamber was fucking empty. Shaun tackled him to the ground and despite Sparky's strength and guile, he managed to knock him senseless as the Thai man's head connected with a small anchor that was conveniently lying on the podium deck. Just in case that hadn't done the trick, Shaun did his best to strangle the life out of Sparky until Frank arrived and pulled him away from the unconscious man.

'Shaun, you are a reckless bastard, you could have been shot!'

At which, Shaun broke down and burst into tears. He'd certainly been through the whole gamut of emotions in the last few days, that much was certain. Then a familiar voice rang through his ears.

'You soppy cunt!'

Debs was back in the land of the living.

Frank handed both of the fugitives to his Police buddies and, after parking the jet-skis back on the beach, drove to the hospital with Shaun and Nok. After parking the car, he looked Shaun in the eye and told him,

'Listen Shaun, you fucked up bad but I think your actions just now have done a lot to get you back on track'. He went on, 'We all make mistakes in this shitty life but it's how we make amends that really matters'.

Shaun didn't reply as he followed Nok into the hospital. When they approached the ward where they had left Jack, Frank left the pair and went to find Chilli.

'Where Jack?' Nok asked as they were faced with an empty ward.

The duty nurse was preparing the bed for whoever was the next occupant and she faced Nok with a world weary and regretful face as she broke the news that Ice had died, then come back to life, and was now undergoing an operation. Both Shaun and Nok had to fight back the tears as she explained how Ice had hung on until she had given birth to Jack's healthy bouncing baby girl. They were then directed to another room where Jack was completely zonked out in the bed next to the cot.

The nurse brought a pair of plastic chairs for them and as Nok went off in search of coffee, Jack started to wake up. He looked at Shaun and let out a huge groan as his mind clicked into gear. It was as if he had just lived through an incredibly sad dream and this was him coming out of the other side.

The duty nurse heard him moving around and quickly scurried into the room looking fairly knackered herself.

'Jack, I am so sorry mate, is this your baby?' Shaun was doing his level best to keep things calm, but it wasn't working.

'I need to go and find the fuckers who did this to Ice'.

Shaun placed his hand on Jack's arm and said,

''It's okay mate, we've got them both'.

Jack scowled and replied,

'It's not fucking okay; you signed her death warrant you prick! She may not live through this surgery. Why would you do this to her? To me?'

Shaun took it on the chin and squeezed Jack's shoulder before going off to find the other person who he had fucked over.

Frank was standing over Chilli, who, thanks to a few shots of tranquilizers, was snoring like a baby seal. Shaun sensed that Frank was having a moment so he stood by the door instead of joining them.

'Now listen Chilli, you don't want to hear this right now, but according to the records I dug up, it looks like I'm your Dad'

Shaun walked in and blurted out, 'What the actual fuck?'

Frank swung round and then back at Chilli.

'Yes I was the irresponsible bastard that gave him up for adoption all those years ago in Wallingford'.

End Game

This was totally off the scale thought Shaun but at least it was less intense than the shitstorm that they'd just experienced.

Turning back to Shaun, with a smile, Frank asked him, 'Shaun, would you like me to fix that sodding tattoo on your arm?'

Less than 30 minutes later, they were both in Frank's favourite Tattoo parlour, Celebrity Ink Pattaya. The entire room burst into laughter as they recognised Frank and his latest victim.

'Oh Frank, you are a badass!'

Shaun looked on sheepishly as he was told that he wasn't the first to have this prank inked into his arm, and he wouldn't be the last.

Opening up the huge selection of designs, the artist started pointing out the ones that would not only erase the current tattoo but also make a meaningful statement that Shaun could wear with some pride for the rest of his life.

'My shout, I'll pick you up in a few hours'. Frank headed back to the hospital with a head full of his own thoughts and future decisions that needed to be made.

End of Chapter Eleven

▲ *Racing Car Girls - Photo by Paul Eddie Yates Photography*

EPILOGUE

For Chilli, Frank, Shaun and Jack, life would never be the same again. Thailand changed them in ways no one could have predicted. Shaun would somehow have to come to terms with his sexuality, whatever that turned out to be.

He'd also not be seeing his sister for a long, long time, no biggie there, as she turned out to be a sado-masochistic bitch, to say the least. He returned to Wallingford and moved into Deb's place, as she wasn't going to use it for the foreseeable future. Shaun found a therapist who he visits twice a week, in an attempt to make sense of the desires he feels towards women, men and ladyboys. He's been into a lot of kinky experimentation on his quest to define his sexual orientation. He gets laid now more than ever before.

Would Frank and Chilli finally go on that well-worn path of being Father and Son, after all of those years apart?

Well, this story isn't really about them.

But yes, they were able to make up for lost time as Chilli was recovering from nine surgeries to repair his legs, and learning how to walk again. Frank smoothed the way for Chilli to slide into the Pattaya bar scene and make some friends of his own. They even work in business together. Thanks to Bryan Flowers of the NightWish Group, they are following his business blueprint and making serious money.

Nok had almost lost her own life and her best friend, and was alive to tell the tale. She is now working as a Mamasan in one of the bars that Jack and Ice own. How did this happen?

Well, when Sparky was sentenced to 25 years in prison, the judge put his holdings up for sale. Jack and Frank pooled their savings and bought six of his bars for a song. They brought Nok on as a Mamasan, and she and Ice watch over the girls and maintain high standards for their customers

Epilogue

and employees. Their bar girls are the most desired in all of Pattaya, and their reputations are well regarded around the globe.

Nok never married, but she and Frank have a 'special' relationship. He can look at the girls in their bars, but can't touch. The magnificent and loyal Nok is at his side, and they are happy.

Debs and Sparky?

She is known in the Thai prison as 'Crazy White Bitch'. She may one day be released and get to see the end of days outside of the jail house. God help us all...

Sparky wasn't as lucky. In jail, he was threatened by many of the men that he had crossed during his rise as a mafia thug, and one night, he met his maker, as his head was removed from his shoulders with an electric wire.

Jack? He's turned into a hero. The stuff legends are made of.

He found the love of his life, and since Christmas Day 2019 when Ice was rolled out of the operating room and saw him and their baby waiting for her, they have never spent a night apart. He used the inheritance from his parents to buy that shrimp farm from Ice's uncle. They split their time between Isaan and Pattaya.

When they need to go back to the city, Ice's sisters babysit baby Chompoo. Yes that's her name .

They named the baby after the sweet delicious fruit that they still enjoy together in bed. Chompoo is a real beauty, and her parents will never let her anywhere near Pattaya.

Remember Noi, the manipulative, thieving, ruthless whore who Jack rode to the finish line as viewed by thousands worldwide? She's laughing all the way to the bank. She now has a cult following and a website. Punters reserve time slots with her in advance and pay to be recorded and uploaded to her homepage where visitors rate the act on a variety of criteria.

She has benefited greatly from the Wallingford stag party.

APPENDIX

Interview with Bryan Flowers the CEO of Night Wish Group

▶ **Hi Bryan, can you tell me a little about your position here in Pattaya and the NightWish group please?**

I founded The Pattaya Addicts Forum in 2006, The Pattaya News in 2017 with Adam Judd, The Night Wish Group in 2012 (we currently have 29 bars and 500 staff while writing this) and I am invested in other businesses and projects around Pattaya. I also consult business owners, donate to charity and fundraise. I love Pattaya and Thai people. Recently I have joined toastmasters in Sri Racha and I am trying to be a key member. I like to write about self-development, business and general ex-pat advice. I love promoting Pattaya and now our businesses.

▶ **How do you see the Pattaya scene developing over the next 5 years or more?**

I think Pattaya will keep expanding and the rents will continue to go up, because I see landlords buying constantly at high prices in the background. I think the nightlife will continue but the areas and the demographics will continuously change, the strongest and hardest business owners will survive. It's important to keep adapting. There will be higher levels of competition in the future and bars will be harder to compete with. The groups of bars will have a key advantage. Those that know how to advertise and brand their businesses will be at a huge advantage, I see many businesses choking their growth by limiting their spend on advertising.

Appendix

- **What advice would you give to first time visitors to Pattaya?**

Someone told me once that Pattaya is like a dream and we should always treat it that way, I don't agree with this mentality because many of us live here, but its good advice for the first few trips. My advice is have a good time and try many places. And to take advice from a collection of people, not a salty expat. There are plenty of groups and forums to get advice from, and don't let anyone tell you what to do with your money. Tipping is totally up to you, if you want to throw some balls in a gogo or ring a bell, then why not. Your first few trips you will remember forever.

- **Do you think it is a good idea for would-be businessmen to try coming over to run a bar or maybe a hotel here in Pattaya?**

I have written about this many times but there was a lot of terms to it, if you are prepared to learn, adapt, listen to people, take your time, don't "hang out", out work your competition and work out your real service/product prices and charge accordingly, you will do well. The key is to offer good value and not market by price.

- **Do the NightWish group have bars in other parts of the country?**

We keep getting asked if we are buying bars in Bangkok. I really haven't done my research into it and Pattaya is our playground. If we do a business in Bangkok, we will need an edge and I will have to consult all my business connections in Bangkok. I won't rule it out, but we do very well dominating sois. There are much better investments in Pattaya and that is where our team live. I am still looking into Cambodia but I see so much potential there because I don't see many business owners applying our strategies and professionalism, many are quite laid back and feel that there is no room to change.

Appendix

▶ **How has the scene changed since the first time you came to Pattaya?**

I did a save soi 6 campaign a year before I got our first bar down there, it was dead, we have raised it to be one of the best soi's in Pattaya. Soi 8 and Soi 7 is far less busy but it's still busy enough. Many of the darkside bars in East Pattaya have suffered since the drink driving clampdown. There is less naughtiness in public and less ST rooms around, but apart from that, everything is still expanding nicely, I think the supply of bars is expanding faster than the demand, but things will balance out later or the weak hands will keep dropping off.

▶ **Do you think that more bar areas in and outside the city limits will develop in the future?**

I think Pattaya will keep expanding and soi Buakhow will get more attention. It's very hard to see the future with the bars here but once central Pattaya is full of real estate, it will start pushing out. As areas become in more demand I see the property guys swooping in, there are many of them just like bar owners, then the high rent makes people buy elsewhere slowly. I see the shifts and it's important to ride the waves or buy on certain sois at the right time. Soi Buakhow rents are going up and the prices of drinks are due an increase, but it needs someone to start the increases, once that happens, you will see more bars pop up and more girls. Despite what a few moaners online think, higher prices helps our scene survive and prosper. If everyone put tons of effort into advertising/promoting like we did, there would be even more people coming to Pattaya.

▶ **Would a first time bar owner in Pattaya need previous business experience?**

I feel that anyone can start a bar in Pattaya but there are many key aspects that would put them at an advantage, not having a limited mindset helps, but you need to work very hard and long hours to get established, many guys cannot leave party mode and they burn out or spend all of their cash.

I always say that Pattaya sorts the men between the boys, I can see them coming and going, they normally last 1-3 years, but it's like watching a train crash over and over. These are the type of guys that usually turn on people around them and blame everything on Pattaya. If you are not happy in Pattaya then I don't think you can be happy anywhere. A few of us have offered consulting services but everyone arrives an expert and convinced themselves that they should save money and not get help, so they normally come to us to be rescued but by then the money pot is empty and it's too late.

It takes a certain type of person to be successful in Pattaya, I would say that experience can help, but it can also hinder. Certainly a marketing background helps.

Bryan Flowers – CEO of Nightwish Group

Appendix

Interview with Paul Eddie Yates – Award winning Street Photographer

▶ **Paul, can you tell the readers about your photography business/hobby here in Pattaya please?**

I retired at 50 as a professional qualified photographer and aimed to cover many self-designed assignments based around street photography…however, after 6 months I was again shooting for local media companies. I know photograph for many companies including worthwhile charities

▶ **I understand you also work as Full Time Tourist Policeman; can you tell me what that involves please?**

Resigned!!! Along with three other expats

▶ **Paul, you are also involved with lots of other interests here in Thailand, would you care to share these with us please?**

N/A

▶ **What do you look for when you are taking a photograph in and around Pattaya?**

Photography is personal to me especially street photography trying to capture candid emotional images. I equally try to inject the same ethos into commercial photography when necessary. Motorsport photography has so many elements from shooting fast moving cars, many beautiful models but ultimately my job is to capture the event for a racing team which involves up to 13 racing cars 21 racing drivers, either professional or gentlemen. In essence there is a myriad of engineers, technicians, support and of course family,

Appendix

friends and supporters which has to be captured and documented... Personally shooting I look for the shock unusual captures which do cause mixed revues...the good the bad and the ugly. However, I don't shoot the vulnerable and homeless

▶ **How would you describe Pattaya to someone who has never been?**

Pattaya is like no other place I have visited and I've visited 125 countries to date. It has a mixture of culture then on the other hand the biggest sex city in the world attracting millions yearly, Thousands of bars and girls in abundance...an adult paradise on steroids.

▶ **Paul could you tell us of some of your proudest moments here please?**

Being allowed to photograph amazing people with such kindness... I have terrific clients who return over and over which is extremely important to me. Personally though I was highly privileged to be part of a Thai team of 36 pro photographers invited to capture the commemoration of the passing of the late Thai King...I was the only foreign officially assigned photographer within the team...Over a 100,000 people attended...Emotions beyond capturing the mourning of their beloved King!

▲ *Dr Martens being polished – Photo by Paul Eddie Yates*

▲ *Paul Eddie Yates*

Appendix

Interview with Chris Stan – Former Bar Manager in Soi 6

- **Hi Chris, hope you are well! Just wanted to ask you a few questions about Pattaya and your job here please**

  Sure, no problem!

- **How long have you lived here?**

  I have travelled to Pattaya for ten years and have lived here for the last two to three years

- **How old are you now?**

  I am now 28 years old

- **How many clubs/bars have you run so far?**

  I have acted as a relief manager for roughly half the time I have been staying here and have probably looked after about 20 bars

- **Do you have any advice for people who want to come over to Pattaya and start their own bar?**

  If you're looking to start your own bar in Pattaya my biggest advice would be pay attention to the way the economics of the city have changed over recent years and try to make sure your branding is targeted at the clientele starting to come to Pattaya rather than what has traditionally been

- **Do you have any regrets about coming to Pattaya?**

  No regrets to be honest I came back multiple times a year for many years before settling here and wouldn't have done so if I didn't love this city

Appendix

▶ **In your opinion, what is the best area/Soi here in Pattaya? And why is that?**

The best area/Soi has so many variables however the way I look at it. Soi 6 is best for those who want a good time for a short time. Soi 7 is my favourite spot when I feel like a game of pool. Soi made in Thailand is a great all round experience with something for everyone. Walking street was my baby back in my teens however I have slowly grown away from it as I get older and I believe many people would be in the same position. Soi Khao Noi on the dark side is my escape street on my days off where I can enjoy nice food and watch my young brothers play football

▶ **What's the funniest/most memorable thing you have seen since living here?**

Funniest moment in Pattaya would be my mate famously known here as Tinka who rung the bell for the 50th time in a single night in my bar in which he pulled the whole thing from the ceiling and decided to add the bell to his outfit from the night

Funniest moment in Thailand overall would have to be on one of my escapes to Koh Chang in which 7 of us rented scooters to explore the island. Everyone assured me they could ride bikes so off we went. The first bend we get to one of my mates fails to turn and crashes into the ditch of what was the local police station no injuries other than his ego

▲ Chris Stan

▲ Chris Stan with some of the Nightwish team

▲ Chris Stan ready for work

▲ Chris Stan with the Envy team

▲ Chris Stan in the Classroom

Appendix

Bar girl Interview

– She is upset – no questions added – just a sample of her feelings after a potential future partner has let her down

- **Thanks for doing this interview, why are you so sad?**

    Today I cried .. tired and very discouraged. Alone .. No one
    Sometimes thought of wanting to quit

- **Why don't you stop working bar?**

    But do not do it .. because I miss mom .. Pity mom. one year from homeland to work. No matter how tired and discouraged .. I will fight. Fight until it's good. In the moment of discouragement, I didn't know what to say to anyone. Only cry in the room alone. It's lonely. When will my life be good ..

- **What keeps you going?**

    I want someone who loves me .. I want to live with the person who loves me. I will find work and help build a family.

- **Does he need to be rich?**

    I do not want rich people. Just love and be honest with me and not forsake me .. that's enough.

    but no. How long have I to cry like this .. I don't know.

- **What happens if you never meet this person?**

    Maybe someone comes into my life

    But without ... I live freely

    Work to make money for my family

In return for the merit of father and mother

▶ **What happens when you don't have money to send home?**

I have to take the car to pawn in order to use the money to spend. I do for him everything. So that he doesn't have to think too much. And he never helped me I'm tired enough. Hopefully, you will understand me.

▶ **Will you find that person here?**

Maybe I wasn't made for anyone. Being free is beautiful. The advantages of being alone - not uncomfortable - Do not be considerate of anyone - Do not wait to care for anyone's feelings - can live alone on no one.

Life has to move on even though someone is missing.

▶ **Do you ever come home alone after working the bar?**

Some days, I have no customers. Without even the money to send to mom. Some days go to work for free .. I want to get the money .. reduced price to 700 baht ... the customer is still not satisfied. Customers need 500 baht.. fuck you I not go.

▶ **I wish you the best and do hope that you can meet that special person**

So tired. How long until I find someone to take me out of here?

▶ **Why do you work here and not in another country?**

After the new year .. I may go to work in a foreign country. Sell service. I'm thinking. I don't have to worry anymore. I come to work in Pattaya because I want to have a foreign boyfriend. But our destiny is not the same.

▶ **All the best for your future**

Some people come to live only for a short time, then there are patrons to look after.

And me .. how long have to wait .. until that day. No one can answer.

▲ *Soi 6 Bar Lady*

PATTAYA 2020

▲ Heaven Above Pattaya

PATTAYA 2020

▲ Dave Samuels of Touch a Gogo

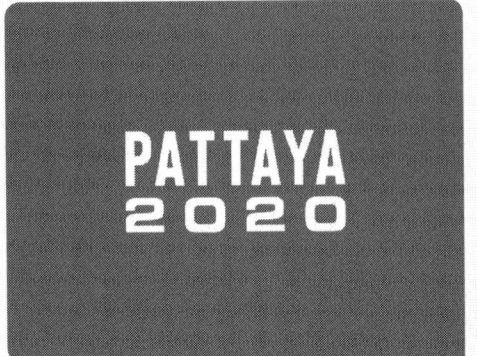

Celebrity Ink - Pattaya

Nightwish Group Ladies of Soi 6

Nightwish Group Ladies of Soi 6

PATTAYA 2020

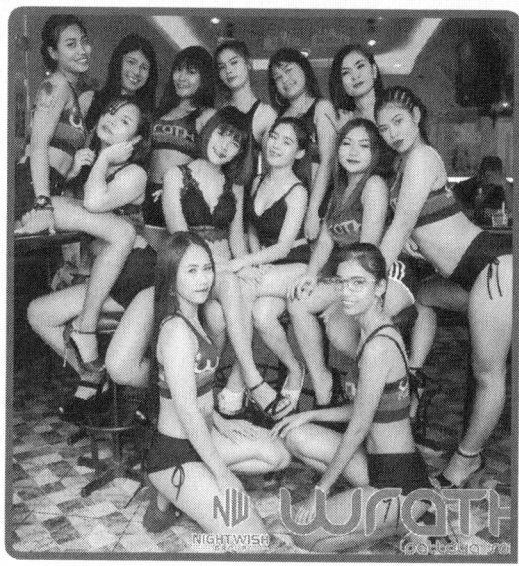

PATTAYA 2020

Nightwish Group Ladies of Soi 6

THANK YOU

A Special Thanks to the following people who made this book possible thanks to their support, enthusiasm, advice, photos and for just being there:

Chris Stan
Bryan Flowers CEO of Nightwish
Group Dave Samuels
Paul Eddie Yates
Stephen Leather
Fernando
Jum Hall
Tom Hall
Cameron Crawford
Celebrity Ink
KD

Also by this Author and available on Amazon

▲ *Wallingford Wishing Well*

▲ *Bangkok to Ben Nevis Backwards*

AUTHOR'S NOTE

As for Pattaya, it's simply a place that you have to experience for yourself to believe. To be fair, it has received some downright terrible press over the last 50 years and I doubt if that stain will ever leave in some people's minds. But I have been there many times, and in my opinion there is nowhere quite like it and if you ever feel like popping over, you really should.

This story is a fictional tale of how many separate lives can be affected when you don't prepare for the consequences of your actions. So it happened in Pattaya but it could have been anywhere, quite literally

Hey, get yourself over to Pattaya in 2020 or 2021 because I guarantee you will be treated well and quite possibly have the best fucking time of your life!

Yours' Sincerely

Phil Hall

If you enjoyed my book please leave a review on my Amazon Author Page:

https://www.amazon.co.uk/Phil-Hall/e/B078V5H9G3?ref=sr_ntt_srch_lnk_1&qid=1586509287&sr=8-1

Also please visit my Facebook Page:

https://www.facebook.com/Phil-Hall-Books-2214571798866344/

www.philhallbooks.co.uk

PATTAYA
2020

Printed in Great Britain
by Amazon